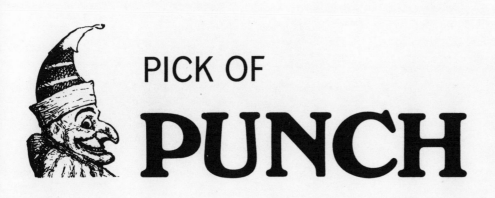

PICK OF
PUNCH

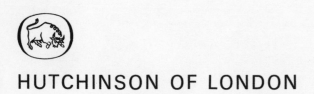

HUTCHINSON OF LONDON

A Punch book, published by
Hutchinson & Co. *(Publishers)* Ltd.
3 Fitzroy Square, London, W.1
London Melbourne Sydney Auckland
Wellington Johannesburg Cape Town
and agencies throughout the world
© 1972 by Punch Publications Limited

Printed in Great Britain by
George Pulman & Sons Ltd.
ISBN 0 09 113010 7

Contents

Introduction

Some reviewers of the last *Pick of Punch* complained that we don't print enough sharp topical satire. *Punch*, they said, was "cosy". This, of course, is the kind of generalisation we have lived with for years—along with that business about dentists' waiting rooms. The simple answer is that we are a weekly magazine and that we *do* print sharp, topical satire. Much of it, though, dates very quickly and does not really belong in an annual anthology. If there was an annual *Pick of the Sunday Times* there wouldn't be a news story in it. If there was an annual *Best of the New Statesman* they would have to leave out all that Labour Party gossip, even if it broke their hearts. If there was a *Pick of the Radio Times* . . .

But we are lucky, because along with the day-to-day sharpshooting we carry a lot of pieces that haven't even begun to date yet. You could simply read it again and laugh as much as you did the first time, without calling it anything at all. Whether it's Country Life, our anthology of life in the provincial press, or Alan Coren attempting to start a Channel swim; whether it's Carl Foreman rewriting High Noon or Jonathan Routh reviewing the A-D Telephone Directory, it's the genuine article and it improves with keeping.

So I have no hesitation in saying that everything in this book is a gem. I am equally convinced that you will find some of the things in this book boring, pointless or in bad taste, because humour is still, even after years of research and laboratory work, a matter of individual taste. Thank goodness. Handing someone a *Pick of Punch* and saying: "Does this amuse you?" is like handing them a menu and asking: "Do you like food?" Ladies and gentlemen, *Punch* is served. Bon appetit.

WILLIAM DAVIS

Pick of Punch

*"You mean we're **all** being hi-jacked? Even in first class?"*

Spaghetti Alla Mafia

By WILLIAM DAVIS

He looked like a worn-out Anthony Quinn—dark-skinned, unshaven, pot-bellied, sad. His eyes were bloodshot, and the hand that raised the half-filled glass of wine was shaky. His jacket was stained with the remnants of countless forgettable meals. His name was Rosario Terrasi, and he was the chief of his local Mafia. Or so the judge in Palermo had said.

"They took me from my eighteen grandchildren," Rosario wailed. "I never even had a chance to say goodbye."

We were on the tiny island of Filicudi, a respectable distance from the east coast of Sicily. Few people had ever heard of the place until Terrasi and fourteen other alleged Mafia chiefs arrived there some weeks ago. They were arrested in a dramatic swoop, and dispatched to Filicudi under the Italian law which permits the banishment of "undesirables" even if they have still to be tried and found guilty. The one hundred and ninety-seven islanders promptly abandoned Filicudi in protest, and returned only when Rome promised to send the Mafiosi men elsewhere. They are now in Sardinia; I was there when the islanders waved them goodbye.

On this hot afternoon, a few days before they left, Terrasi was sitting outside the Hotel Sirene. The Sirene has seen better days, but that isn't saying much. As we talked, the other Mafiosi joined us one by one. They were bored, and we offered a break in a dreary routine.

To understand the Sicilian Mafia (whose influence is almost entirely confined to the western part of the island) one has to accept several basic facts: the long history of corruption, the widespread distrust of officialdom, the poverty of much of the population, the superstitions of ignorant peasants, the Sicilian's devoted pursuit of power through fear, and the deep-rooted belief that real strength lies in loyalty to family and friends. Sicilian pride is often absurd, and violence lies close to the surface, but the Mafia continues to exist because it is based on a way of life. Mario Puzo's best-seller, *The Godfather,* is set in America, and the America of several decades ago at that. But Don Corleone is impressively real. "Does this man have real balls?" he asks his *Consigliori* before tackling a rival, and Puzo explains what he means: does he have the courage to risk everything, to take a chance on losing all on a matter of principle, on a matter of honour; for revenge? The *Consigliori* is made to put it another way: "You're asking if he is a Sicilian."

I did not find it difficult to visualise the fifteen Mafia men of Filicudi as the entire cast of *The Godfather.* Even Terrasi, despite his unimpressive appearance, fitted in. He was less smooth than his city colleagues, but one could see him oozing sentimentality one minute and being utterly callous the next. If someone got hurt, he would smile sweetly and explain that it was entirely the victim's fault: he shouldn't have got in the way. The others looked even more convincing. There was Calogero Sinatra (yes!), a sly, intelligent-looking man who looked capable of anything. And Giacomo Coppola, a thick-set aggressive type proudly displaying an immensely hairy chest. And Antonio Buccelato—a short, powerfully built Sicilian who shouted every word and underlined his arguments with swift karate chops that made the heavy table tremble. And a quiet, white-haired man who wouldn't give his name, but told me in excellent English that he despised the communists but adored the late Winston Churchill "because he knew what he wanted, and got it." And a slim George Raft type who, despite the heat, was immaculately dressed. And an old man with a limp who appeared harmless until my companion, a photographer from Milan, suggested that he was lucky to be in Filicudi because the sun was shining and the sea was wonderfully blue. The old man suddenly turned violent and lashed out with

"The Americans get Bob Hope . . ."

"It's their unpredictable weather that I like."

his walking stick. For fully ten minutes he heaped abuse on the world, and the Italian Government in particular. He had been arrested by mistake, he hated the place, they wouldn't let him see a doctor, there was no justice, and all journalists were swine. He would make everyone pay for it as soon as he got home.

It was all very convincing. But, of course, appearances can be deceptive. I always thought that Humphrey Bogart and Jack Palance made utterly convincing villains—more so than, say, Al Capone. And the head of the police force guarding the Mafiosi confessed, with a grin, that when a foreign television crew had found it difficult to get enough Mafia men together for an interview, he had stepped into the breach. Who, after all, would know the difference?

Coppola and Buccelato invited us inside the hotel for a beer, and for the next two hours we had a heated discussion. There wasn't a policeman in sight, except for the obliging commandant, dressed in sweat shirt and an old pair of trousers. "We can't," he explained, "have policemen walking up and down in the sun." Buccelato nodded agreement. "We and the police," he said, "understand each other." He went on to claim that he'd been arrested because he was making a lot of money, and people were jealous. He was a nice chap really, a family man whose brother was a Monsignore. How could anyone possibly think that he was a Mafioso? "There is no Mafia in Sicily," he declared. "They only use it as an excuse." He was "like a little stone thrown into a well." He couldn't claim to be an angel, but if he and the others were really Mafiosi they wouldn't be in Filicudi. "The real Mafia is

"Who's the stranger riding in with Tom?"

sitting behind beautiful desks, with servants opening their doors for them," he said. "If you want to find the true Mafia bosses, look at the closest friends of politicians."

Coppola (accused of being involved in an American drug ring) also claimed that they were being offered up as a sacrifice. "If they make a show of arresting people like us from time to time," he said, "they can leave the real villains alone." He was bitter about the islanders who, he said, had been "very insulting." They were treating them like monsters. "Children run away from us," he said. "I tried to offer one some money and his mother pulled him away. One small boy even asked me if it was true that we eat children. My God, we have children of our own!"

Buccelato said it was high time that the Government formed a body which could establish what a Mafioso is. Was a man who took bribes, in return for awarding someone a profitable contract, a Mafioso or just a clever business-man? Was a fellow who got into a fight, in order to defend the family honour, a Mafioso or merely a decent, upright Sicilian? Was a corrupt poli-tician who used his office to advance his own interests a Mafioso, or simply a man who recognised that if you don't look after yourself in this harsh world, no one else would do it for you? "If Jesus had been born in Palermo," he added, "he would have been a Mafioso too." He hit the table to emphasise his point, and ordered another round of beer. We could see that they were really quite decent fellows, couldn't we? Did we think they were capable of killing people? They loved their little children, and missed their homes. They had been unfairly treated, because Italy wasn't a civilised country. It couldn't happen anywhere else in the world.

We finished our beer (the eager hotel proprietor insisted that it was "on the house") and said goodbye. Eight of the Mafiosi insisted on accompany-ing us to our boat. "Come again tomorrow night," they said. "We'll get some fish and cook dinner." The commandant nodded agreement, and they all waved until our boat was out of sight.

Around the corner, on the other side of the island, some of the local tradesmen confessed that they would miss the Mafiosi. There had been a lot of talk about Filicudi losing tourist trade, but the truth was that there had

12

never been much of it anyway. They had put up a sign "Tourism is our bread" for the benefit of television crews. The Mafiosi had done for Filicudi what Ingrid Bergman had done for Stromboli. Millions of people around the world had heard of Filicudi for the first time. They would come to see where the Mafia chiefs had stayed. And they would eat spaghetti alla Mafia—a new dish just invented by the best cook in Filicudi (garlic, parsley, oil and red pepper). Who knows, one might even be able to sell some Mafia souvenirs.

The Mafia chiefs, they went on, were not really such bad fellows. Some of the islanders actually regarded them as heroes—though, of course, it didn't pay to say so. Look how many policemen it had taken to bring them to Filicudi!

We tasted the spaghetti alla Mafia, and decided that the tradesmen were right. The protests had been unnecessary; Filicudi had collected a fortune's worth of publicity. We also decided that, if Mafia meant corruption, the world was full of Mafiosi. The Mafia was, in Barzini's phrase, a "many-headed dragon" and bigger heads than Terrasi's and Buccelato's were going free. Not least, we reflected that the most effective weapon against secret organisations like the Mafia is ridicule. The Mafia's power depends on fear. Make them look big, and you enhance their prestige. Laugh at them, and people will laugh with you.

"Now here's a song about ecology and environmental pollution . . ."

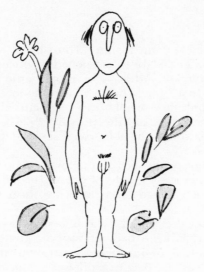

In the Beginning

Man's clothes-sense

was simply a way

ffolkes' History of ffashion

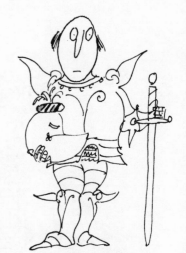

of ornament

he has never ceased

to find

new answers

of keeping warm but   as the years rolled by   he discovered in himself   a certain love

and display just   for the sheer hell of it.   In his endless pursuit   of the fair sex

until we come   to the present century   when he seems to be only   just beginning.

Underneath the

★★

★★

The Duke of Windsor, as King Edward VIII, was glamorous; the Queen isn't. Apart from his brilliance in weightier forms, Pierre Trudeau has glamour measurable in megatons; even with his yachting cap on, it is doubtful if an artesian rotary-bore could locate any in Edward Heath. Mick Jagger, an indifferent rock singer, generates around himself a magnetic field of it; although surrounded by all the TV spectacular apparatus, Cilla Black hasn't a spark. James Bond has glamour; Sean Connery hasn't.

All racing motorists have got it, but no golf champions. She will probably cut me up for pointing it out, but Germaine Greer is G; strive though she might, Jacqueline Susan is non-G. Lord Beaverbrook had it in electric quantities; Lord Thomson of Fleet probably couldn't care less, which is okay, as he hasn't. Nureyev has it to an intense degree; Margot Fonteyn is without it. Air hostesses and Sinatra used to have it but no longer do; Tom Jones has a coarse-grained sort.

Bunny Girls, who are supposed to be loaded, have no more glamour than

16

Arclights....

★★★

★★★

a doughnut; Manson's Family had it in a horrible way. Castro has it, histrionically, but all the US astronauts put together didn't have a dab. Noel Coward has gone on getting more and more glamorous; poor Ivor Novello, although he thought he had it and wrote shows called *Careless Rapture* and *Glamorous Night*, was too damp to have it. George Best is rotten with it. No TV link-men and reporters have it: they are too drably familiar at the fireside circle. Even Alan Whicker, whose favourite subject it is, is mundanely unglamorous. Upon being sent to do time Bernard Falk unexpectedly acquired it, but it may not last.

It may be seen that there is no justice about glamour. It doesn't necessarily cohabit with talent or worth, although neither are they automatically precluded by its possession. Also it must be distinguished from charisma and stardom. Charisma comes from within, whereas glamour is bestowed from without—by the public with the help of the PR industry. For instance, we all thought President Kennedy had charisma but he may have had only glamour. On the other hand, Tommy Steele has no glamour but has bags of

17

star quality. Raquel Welch has glamour like children have measles. The super Glenda Jackson isn't glamorous and who cares?

Nowadays glamour hasn't much to do with how you evaluate people, either philosopher-kings or your personal fancy. It seems ineluctably old fashioned. Would any child of our time of the Alternative Society want to be described as glamorous? She would probably stare with baffled, stony eyes suspecting that you were putting her on. It would be like telling her she was curvaceous, or had plenty of this and that, or was a looker or a kayo Katy, one-time compliments which are now also almost meaningless. Glamour isn't quite so obsolete but drained from it is the import of desirability of a dazzling but unattainably celestial kind.

When I was a randy lad my friends and I talked about glamorous girls all the time, but we didn't actually know any. "I say, man," (like Blossom Dearie, we even called our girl friends man, but we were no finger-snapping hipsters: this manning was in the spirit of cricket field manliness)—"I say, man, how about that for glamour," we would mutter urgently, covertly nodding across the Ace of Spades swimming pool on a Sunday afternoon and mooning miserably at some suburban 23-year-old who seemed cut out of a picture palace screen, eyebrows like crow's talons, mouth a glace cherry, poker-faced and invulnerable. Or again, as we self-consciously did the Big Apple to "The Flat-Foot Floogie with the Floy Floy" at a Saturday night hotel dance, across the Judy Garlandish hair-dos of the local tennis club girls we furtively breathed in the fumes of glamour radiating from a Great West Road Hedy Lamarr. She would be older than our 17-year-old cousins

"Notice the rickety staircase, the uneven sloping floors, the walls out of alignment . . ."

". . . and two long range weather forecasters. That's the lot."

and their convent school chums, all bobbysox and hockey stick bruises, and she would have been brought from some metropolitan Kubla Khan pleasure dome like Barons Court in a Hudson Terraplane by a suave dog-track punter in a maroon bow tie and with the slightly thicker toothbrush moustache Clark Gable had grown for *Gone With The Wind.* Glamour subsisted upon the sort of sickly chastity and hopeless masochistic yearning troubadours cultivated in their unconsummated love for their Ladies of Pain: medieval glamourpusses.

Within a few years glamour was being devalued. It was being wallpapered by press agents and caption-writers over any starlet, oomph girl or sweater girl used for cheesecake and pin-ups in the early '40s. It became wretchedly diluted and thumbed over. That's when glamour-puss came in, along with glamour queen and even glamourette. It deteriorated to a smear: when sturdy infantrymen put the label Glamour Boys (as a change from Brylcreem Boys) upon those effeminates who rode around in RAF bombers.

Of course the word isn't done for (not long ago the American publication, *Glamor,* was still running such endearing features as "10 Best Dressed College Girls") but it's exhausted unto inaction. Conducting some disordered research, I checked out *Vogue* and reports on Cecil Beaton's autumn fashion anthology at the Victoria and Albert, I looked through *Woman* and followed Felicity Green in the *Mirror,* I examined the Eurofashion '71 plans and cased William Hickey; although the *Daily Mail's* Suzy Knickerbocker column referred to "groovy debs," "best families," "birds" and "dollies," declared that "London is where it's at" and specifically named the particular " 'in' spot for London's beautiful people" (a " 'now' discotheque"), not a mention about glamour, the derelict cast-off. I did come across it just twice, both times for period atmosphere. Brigid Keenan was reporting in *The Observer* from Los Angeles about a store specialising in pornokitsch underwear, "those curious 'glamour' items you often see in small ads, see-through baby-doll nighties, naughty negligees and cheeky knickers, panties embroidered 'Eeny, meeny, miny moe, this is as far as you can go.'" You can see the spiritual skid-row where glamour's landed. I noticed, too, in a teenagers' mag an advertisement for rainwear. "The styles are more sophisticated and"—there it was—"glamorous." You know why? Because "They are the kind of clothes that Marlene Dietrich, Joan Crawford and Greta Garbo would have worn had they been designed earlier." That's how it is with glamour now. Like nostalgia, it ain't what it used to be.

One of Roy Lichtenstein's mock strip blow-ups, *My Reverie* (1966) is of a pageboy'd blonde with raspberry lips and wistfully lidded eyes sighing into a stick mike "The melody haunts my reverie . . ." That was the 1931 hit, Hoagy Carmichael's "Stardust," with its vague musings of garden walls and hot tropic nights: surrogate romance for that Neolithic Age when there was a depression and no package tours and only Amy Johnson took to the air. Personally even I was a bit too young then to be mass-suggested by the mode. It caught me at the "Deep Purple" point ("sleepy garden walls" again), 1939's most moaned song, by sax sections of such bands as Horace Heidt and Guy Lombardo's Royal Canadians and crooned by Russ Columbo in the bel canto baroque to be maximised by Bing Crosby. The most saturating influence upon the pre-war young was the mythologised image of America and American life. It came via the local Odeon and also BBC wireless, for through the chinks in the Reithian granite oozed Tin Pan Alley fantasies in relays from Belgravia and Piccadilly night clubs. The combined effect was of an endless cabaret scripted by Michael Arlen, a ritzy cosmopolitan supper club, a distant phosphorescence of crepe-de-chine, hair oil and champagne bubbles. You could spoon up the glamour with a gumboot. There was nothing arousingly sexy about those oddly fictional women in duplexes for the entire invention had the artificiality of candied fruit, sugary but with a touch of arsenic in it.

As far as I know, the term glamour cropped up originally in a lyric in Gershwin's "'S Wonderful" (one of his marvellous galaxy for *Girl Crazy* (1930) which included also "Embraceable You" and "But Not For Me," and which introduced both Ethel Merman and Ginger Rogers to Broadway). You'll remember why 's wonderful: "You made my life so glamorous/You can't blame me for feeling amorous." The reason such experiences were welcome by proxy was that most people's lives weren't glamorous, but were bleak and broke. It seems likely that it was Maury Paul, writer of the "Cholly Knickerbocker" gossip column for the Hearst chain, who picked up the word and applied it to Brenda Frazier and the New York cafe society precursors of the jet set we've come to know so deadly well. Up to about then—since it had been lifted by Sir Walter Scott from the Scandinavian (declares the OED)—it had kept the cynical twist it had taken on around the 1840s to connote a magical charm with a hint of hocus-pocus, a mountebank allure. That tarnish was polished off in the mid-'30s, and from then for five years or so it meant the nimbus radiated by the indestructibly gay and rich: the silver glint of money and magnificent dentistry. That's about where my generation came in. While the real '30s tobogganed through the mud of the Slump down toward war, the let's-pretend '30s were manufactured by MGM and the Savoy Orpheans.

I have a theory that glamour, as spread abroad in the '30s and early '40s, was formulated in a novel which sold 1,392 copies when it appeared in 1932 and which described New York (where at sidewalk level ex-stockbrokers lined up with ex-labourers at free soup kitchens) as a fairytale city where "the tops of the buildings shine like the crowns of gold-leaf kings in conference." Before she published *Save Me The Waltz*, and before the '29 Crash, Scott Fitzgerald's wife, Zelda, hit the nerve in an article about Park Avenue,

"*. . . and you will be charged with not trying to bribe a police officer.*"

20

"where one may buy an apple with as much ritual as if it were the Ottoman Empire, or a limousine as carelessly as if it were a postage stamp," and in 1934 she recalled seeing a cafe's lights ". . . shimmer glamorously behind the silhouette of retrospective good times when we still believed in summer hotels and the philosophies of popular songs."

Save Me The Waltz was criticised for its "glittering surface smartness," and indeed that was exactly what was everywhere being hastily pasted over those fearsome cracks in the floorboards: glamour was squirted around like Polyfilla. I'd never heard of Zelda or Scott, and by 1937 there was much talk in the sixth form about leaving school and joining the International Brigade, and we quoted Auden on love needing "death, death of the grain, our death/Death of the old gang." All the same, the philosophy of popular songs was something we simultaneously believed in. They infiltrated seductively. You'd imagine that they must have been a Communist plant, to rub in the mess of a failed capitalist system. But no, it was the sumptuary process of giving the breadline a consoling lip-wettener of luxury as it went on shufflin' along. It's amazing how many of the lyrics were about get-away sun-tanned couples who'd presumably skipped out of the way of the falling ceiling with lots of bullion and jumped a liner for frangipani places. "Sand in my shoes/Sand from Havanna"; "When they begin the beguine . . . down by the shore an orchestra's playing"; "An airline ticket to romantic places"; "Thanks for the memory/Of nights in Singapore"; "In some secluded rendezvous/That overlooks the avenue . . . Cocktails for two."

That was the setting: visuals supplied by Hollywood, as in *Top Hat*, the all-white apartments with round all-white beds and round fluffy all-white rugs on polished floors, and round all-white girls to go in them. Millions peeped in, from the universal servants' quarters and were temporarily warmed by the bright lights and taken by the wryness of the blase, brittle words Cole Porter wrote for them. What a life they had, those gods and goddesses in the Great Penthouse in the Sky. Busby Berkeley's monstrous bouquets of cuties sprouted to the ineffably Manhattany music of Irving Berlin, while Fred Astaire, elegantly streamlined in tails as a swallow a-wing, and twirling Ginger with him, an airy bundle of fun, went twinkling up staircases of black glass to—where? Why, to some rainbow place beyond reality's reach, where all things nasty melted in the blinding glare of glamour.

It's always stayed for me at that 30-year-old point, that hoary bamboozlement. You couldn't lightly risk coming down from a high like that. Or should we start buffing it up, in case we need to call on it again?

"Wow, this is really too much, man —you coming here to rescue a mere boy like me."

A Guide to Motorway Madness

By KEITH WATERHOUSE

General

104.   Motorways are dual-carriageway roads which may not be used by certain kinds of road user; for example, Sunday drivers, women drivers, nervous drivers, or any vehicle with a pushchair on the roof-rack or a small bobbing dachshund in the rear window.

105.   Traffic travels faster on motorways than on ordinary roads, and you will need to sum up traffic situations quickly. The ability to flash your lights, swerve, skid, accelerate, brake, blow your horn and scream, "When are you going to take your bleeding test, then?", all in one fifteenth of a second, is doubly important on motorways.

106.   Make sure your vehicle is fit to cruise at speed, and that the horn which plays the opening bars of "D'ye ken John Peel" is correctly tuned.

Joining the motorway

107.   To join the motorway you will need to be proposed and seconded by two other members, who will normally be found discussing the breathalyser test in the saloon bar of that pub with the plastic thatch just off the slip-road. The password is: "Am I all right for Slagchester?" to which the response will be a sharp intake of breath, a slow shaking of heads and the reply: "You'll have to go back forty miles and get on the M4. The only way

GRAHAM *On a Wing and a Prayer*

"Height thirty thousand feet, flying time four and a half hours . . . we hope you will enjoy your flight."

"If there's nothing to worry about, why do they play this soothing music just before take-off?"

to Slagchester from here is on the B6493." If you say, "Oh, goody, I'm still on the right track, then," you are automatically blackballed.

108.   Never reverse into the motorway or cross the central reserve, unless by doing so you can top your brother-in-law's anecdote about doing a crafty U-turn just outside Coventry.

109.   If you find that you are heading away from where you want to go, as will usually be the case, you must carry on until you reach the next exit. This will take you to a roundabout where you will find a number of RAC signs reading: "Polo at Windsor Great Park." If you are not interested in horseflesh, ask again.

Lane discipline

110.   After joining the motorway, stay in the inside lane long enough to observe bitterly to your passenger that she would think, would she not, that if they were going to allow coal lorries in the middle lane they might as well go the whole hog and let in gypsy caravans.

111.   On a two-lane carriageway, drive on the outside lane except when overtaking. Sound horn and make V-sign when overtaking on nearside.

112.   A goods vehicle with an unladen weight of more than three tons may not use the outside lane. This means that if you are driving on the goods vehicle's tail, and the goods vehicle brakes abruptly, it is the goods vehicle's fault.

113.   Many accidents on wet or icy roads, or in fog, are caused by drivers having forgotten their St Christopher Medallions. Bear in mind also that it is often difficult to cross the fingers while wearing driving gloves.

Overtaking

114.   Overtaking only on the right, unless traffic is moving in queues in all lanes and the fathead in front, who would clearly be happier in a bath-chair, is bumbling along at 70 mph. In these circumstances you may mutter, "Come on, come on, come on," and belt past on the hard shoulder.

115.   Always use mirror and then signal before you move out. Remember: *Mirror—Up you too—Move out.*

116.   You are not supposed to accelerate when being overtaken. On the

"Nervous?... Me?"

"You're already worrying about the flight back, aren't you?"

"I think I'll wait for you here."

other hand, if you do accelerate you will not be overtaken, so you can scrub round this rule entirely.

Warning signals

117. Warning signals consist of a sort of panel with several amber or red lights and the odd computer-type symbol as found on electricity bills. When the lights are flashing you are supposed to turn to your passenger and ask: "What was all that about?" Do not reduce speed.

118. An exclamation mark in a triangle means that you should commence to curse and swear at all those yellow tip-up lorries which are trundling earth from one side of the motorway to the other.

119. The "single lane—no overtaking" sign means that the motorway is littered with squashed plastic bollards for three miles ahead.

Stopping and parking

120. Do not stop except:

   (a) in an emergency (for example, when you are half-way up the back end of a goods vehicle with an unladen weight of more than three tons);

   (b) when invited by the police to breathe in this bag;

   (c) to ask the party of picnickers on the hard shoulder whether they imagine themselves to be in Epping bloody Forest or what.

Leaving the motorway

121. If you are not going to the end of the motorway you will leave by the slip-road on your left. Having ignored the "Get in lane" signs, you will of course be on the outside lane. Before you execute a 90 degree turn at 100 mph, ask yourself *why* you are not going to the end of the motorway. If it is absolutely imperative to be in Slough or wherever, sound your horn while plunging over the flyover.

122. If you miss your turn-off point you must carry on until you reach the next one. The expression, "Ah well, all roads lead to Rome, I suppose," is good for blood-pressure in these circumstances.

123. A post with three chevrons on it, rather like US Army good conduct stripes, is the signal to start arguing about whether you are going to leave the motorway for a cup of coffee. A post with two chevrons on it means that your passenger had better make her mind up in double-quick time. A post with one chevron on it means that she damn well should have said so earlier.

124. When you leave a motorway, remember to check your watch against the mileage. If you have done London to Birmingham in 45 minutes, you are the winner so far.

"Trust people! Trust people! You sound like my other psychiatrist."

HOTEL MIRAMAR
(unfinished)
by LARRY

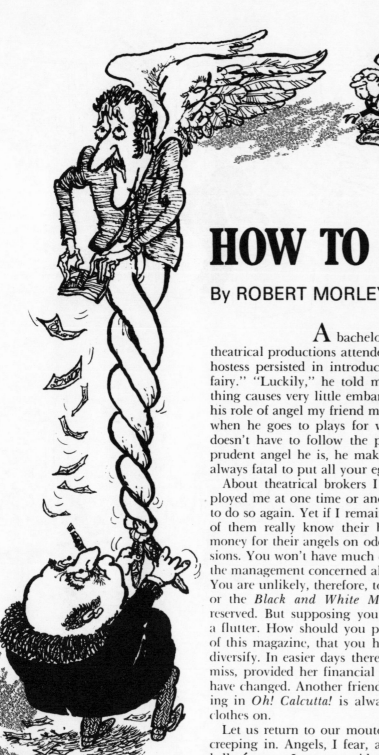

HOW TO BE AN ANGEL

By ROBERT MORLEY

A bachelor friend of mine who persistently invests in theatrical productions attended a cocktail party the other evening, where his hostess persisted in introducing him to all and sundry as a "professional fairy." "Luckily," he told me when recounting the incident, "that sort of thing causes very little embarrassment nowadays." I don't know whether in his role of angel my friend makes money, but at least it gives him an interest when he goes to plays for which he has provided some of the bread. He doesn't have to follow the plot. He can be counting the house. Like the prudent angel he is, he makes a point of spreading his wings. It is nearly always fatal to put all your eggs in one basket.

About theatrical brokers I must write carefully. Most of them have employed me at one time or another, and I am always mindful they may have to do so again. Yet if I remain true to Punch I must point out that very few of them really know their business. That is not to say they won't make money for their angels on odd occasions, but it will always be the odd occasions. You won't have much chance of getting in on the ground floor unless the management concerned already suspects there is a flood in the basement. You are unlikely, therefore, to be asked to invest in a Palladium pantomime or the *Black and White Minstrel Show*. Such rich pastures are strictly reserved. But supposing you have a few pounds to invest and would like a flutter. How should you proceed? I am assuming, since you are a reader of this magazine, that you haven't a mistress whose talent you propose to diversify. In easier days there was always a place in the chorus for a pretty miss, provided her financial backing was in order, but times and choruses have changed. Another friend of mine whose belle amie is currently appearing in *Oh! Calcutta!* is always boasting of how pretty she looks with her clothes on.

Let us return to our moutons, and apologise for the French which keeps creeping in. Angels, I fear, are constantly associated in my mind with the belle époque. Let us consider where your money is, if not safe—that would be asking too much—at least with a chance of survival, and even multiplying. Should you go for the big spender who at the first hint of your interest, the first sight of your cheque book, wines and dines you at Burke's or Scotts or the Grand Véfour? "Steady with the Chateau Lafite," you tell yourself, "this chap will spend the ready in pre-production expenses. He will be back to demand the company's rail fare to Southsea." At least you will have a better time in his company than you will with one of the more austere brethren who lives in a poky little attic on top of his theatre, with

26

minimal furniture and mature lady typists. "No room here," you tell yourself, "for the casting couch," and you are right. If caution reassures you, go for one of these. To my mind you might as well have your money in a building society for all the fun you are likely to get out of it. You will, of course, be sent tickets for the first night, but you will also be expected to pay for them. No, what you need, when you are starting out on your journey along the celestial way, is a little man who has the time—because until he has got your cheque in his bank account, business isn't all that brisk—to show you round the stables, and introduce you to some of the colts and possibly fillies. He may even encourage you to read some scripts and get your advice on the casting, enquiring whether you would prefer Larry or Paul, and when you express surprise that either of these gentlemen is available, you will be further surprised to learn that he gave both of them their first job, and that they would do anything for him, if asked.

Eventually, if you have taken my advice and your cheque has been cleared, you may find yourself invited to a pre-production party to meet the actors who are about to rehearse your play. You will find that not only Olivier and Scofield are missing, but that you have never heard of a single member of the cast. The mood on these occasions is one of hysterical over-confidence. In the abandoned ballroom in which the first rehearsal is to take place, you are uncertain where to put down your emptied champagne glass, and are probably still clutching it as you tiptoe away, unwilling to interrupt the proceedings any longer. If this lot can get away with it, you tell yourself, it will be a miracle. But in the role of angel you should expect miracles. They are not likely, but you should expect them.

Depending on the size of your investment and the amount of spare time and cash you still have available, you may attend the world premiere of the piece, when it opens in Cheltenham, and be amazed how little excitement is generated on this auspicious occasion. You will have to be constantly telling yourself that from little acorns mighty oak trees grow, if you wish to keep up your courage. Monday night is never very brisk in the provinces, and nothing alerts your would-be theatre-goer in the tall grass and persuades him to leave his car in the garage and himself in the parlour more than that fatal announcement on the bills "Prior to immediate London production." Granted that Cheltenham is not exactly the right venue for the piece, and it is unlikely to be properly understood by the natives, everyone agrees afterwards at a party held in the local bistro, that there were one or two good

early laughs and the play held up even if the audience didn't. It needs cutting, the management insist. Cutting is the panacea invariably prescribed after a first night, even if it isn't always applied to the patient. Managements insist on cutting, just as at one time physicians insisted on bleeding. Most plays are sickly at birth, and many succumb at a surprisingly early age. Euthanasia is by no means uncommon, but no such fate awaits your little piece, apparently. After Cheltenham, a week at Bognor is planned and then there is talk of Richmond, immediately prior to its arrival in the West End. After Richmond, however, it suddenly decides to go to Southsea. It seems that the London theatre cannot yet be announced to the impatient West End patrons, as the play currently playing there still refuses to complete two consecutive weeks below its stop figure. But everyone confidently expects it to fold once the Motor Show is over. Southsea comes and goes, and then rather surprisingly Billingham, and by now you are in overcall, that is to say the original subscribed capital having been exhausted by unexpectedly heavy losses on the road, everyone is expected to divvy up again. You are absolutely sick of the play, and just when you are hoping you have heard the last of it, the phone rings and your manager is on the blower to tell you he has a West End theatre and all signals are "Go, go," but there is the question of a further overcall, and will you be sure to let him know how many seats you want for the First Night, and the rush is on. He also apologises in advance for the fact that some of your party may have to be accommodated in the Circle. You tell him that your party will consist simply of your wife and yourself, and what with all the money you have spent already you couldn't possibly afford more than two seats in the Upper Circle. But on this occasion the seats are free, it seems, and when yours arrive you will find you have been accommodated with eight pairs of stalls. You have considerable difficulty getting rid of them. On the whole, perhaps it would be better if you stayed at home that night yourself. If you do decide to attend, you will be in for a shock. First Nights are not what they were. The prevailing mood can be likened to that of a first class railway carriage whose passengers are not expecting the ticket collector to come along. Except for the critics, a faceless coterie of railway employees travelling first because it is one of the perks, no one appears to be exactly at ease. Here and there the season ticket holders add a little reassurance and there is a sprinkling of the more flamboyant characters in showbiz, some of them in evening dress, or what passes for evening dress nowadays if you have time to puzzle it out. There must surely be a man who designs clothes for such occasions, a sort of Teddy Tinling of the centre foyer. The play is received ecstatically. You leave the theatre telling yourself that you are in the money, and the next morning the critics tear it to shreds while the management is busy tearing their notices to shreds to extract a few quotes to paste up outside the theatre. When the play comes off in a month, the final balance sheet shows a deficit of £78, but it seems you are not to be asked to fork out any further sum, and you breathe a sigh of relief and send the letter on to your accountant. You might have done worse. After all, it takes a long time to learn to play the harp.

ROBERT ROBINSON

Aimin', Shootin' and Missin'

By ROBERT ROBINSON

"I daresay you know the sort," said the other customer in the gun shop, "blazes away at low-flying pheasants. Dammit, if you're going to call that sport you might as well stay at home and take pot shots at the Rhode Island Reds on the Home Farm."

A salesman, who looked a bit like Arthur Treacher, placed himself at a sporting distance from me, clasped his hands behind his back, and rocked gently up and down on his heels. What I'd heard made me feel I was in deeper water than I'd been banking on, because up till then it wasn't low-flying pheasants I'd aimed at, so much as ones that had actually landed—birds going for strolls on the A30—and my weapon had been the motor-car. Several times I'd had my wheels up a gassy bank, trying to down one of the succulent creatures with a left and right from the near-side hub-cap. I got rather hot in the face, and the other customer looked at me narrowly.

"I—er—hear that guns from Czechoslovakia aren't bad—" There was a crash as the other customer dropped his matched Purdies. He shied as he hurried out of the door, scenting a parvenu.

Arthur Treacher smiled. "Werl." He fetched a gun out of the rack, hefting it in one hand like a butcher wondering whether to give you the scraps for nothing, or charge you fourpence.

"Hear that?" he said, as he opened and closed the action with a flourish. "Just like a dustbin-lid going back on. Look at the carving on the grip. Probably done with a knife and fork by an old lady living in the Carpathian Hills. They do it like granny does her knitting, watching the telly at the same time. I wouldn't use that gun,"

Arthur Treacher said, bringing to a close this lightning tour of his similes and prejudice, "for anything but spreading ready-mixed cement."

I dashed off to Scotland Yard to expediate the licence, scooped up the gun from Arthur who condescended to receive payment for it, and bore it off to the country feeling dreadfully potent.

"Is that what you take when you go out *killing*, Dad?" my four year old daughter asked, profoundly approving. With some unction I explained that I wasn't going to kill anything I didn't mean to eat, a red herring which suitably obscured the more basic question whether my

"Our only hope is another postal strike!"

29

standard of marksmanship would not for ever protect me from such a moral dilemma: obscured it, I should say, from all save my son, a boy of eleven with a touch of the sphinx about him, who offered to consume unaided anything I hit, up to and including water-buffalo.

Actually, I wasn't terribly interested in bringing anything down, only in the possibility. I don't like going for walks in the country because it is so easy to turn round and go home

again that you can't help wondering whether it's worthwhile setting out in the first place. There are no *limits* in the business of going for walks—rather like golf: you hit the ball, and if it doesn't go far enough you just hit it again, and if that doesn't work you hit it again, and so on, with nothing to make you feel that fewer strokes, rather than many, really matter (whereas with tennis, hit the ball wrong, and the mistake comes back at you over the net). I thought a gun might lend consequence to a walk, it might be an object round which a walk could accumulate, and you'd find yourself doing uncomfortable things like climbing through hedges and getting brambles in your eye without it ever occurring to you—as it always does when you're just out for a stroll—that you don't have to.

I had this vague idea that it was pigeons I was going to slaughter—the only pheasant in our neck of the woods being an ancient bird who each night marched bad-temperedly into the hen-house at Lower Farm, pushed a hen off its perch, and roosted asthmatically in its place till dawn. But in the light of me having to eat everything I shot, I wasn't too happy about it being pigeon—when did you last choose pigeon at a restaurant? Answer, never, on the grounds that you know it's going to chew like elastic-bands. And I had a premonition that if I did manage to down one, it would turn out to be not a woodpigeon, but one of those unshaven meths-drinking Trafalgar Square birds, drying out in the country for the weekend.

But I was committed to shooting at something edible, and I set off with my special country hat (wrested from the head of a man I met driving a yoke of oxen down Bond Street), slid unhandily over the wall at the end of the garden, and started across the meadow to the copse below. The buttercups had barely stained the tops of my wellies when I heard a sound I knew—a derisive rasp, a tinny trumpeting—and there in the lane at the side of the field I saw the hideous moustachioed face of the man they call The Pill, blowing rudely into one of those tin cigars which make a noise like a comb-and-paper.

I'd been wrong-footed by this chap from the moment I'd had the bad luck to run across him relieving himself against my wall as though he were doing the flints a favour. Indeed, he had so much the air of conferring ducal status, that I found myself sneaking through my own garden gate as though my credentials wouldn't bear inspection. Just A Minute, Just A Minute, he roared, buttoning up and approaching me like a gamekeeper who'd copped a poacher. He let me off with a caution that time, and withdrew

"One of the hardest winters in living memory."

playing Colonel Bogy on his lousy gazooka. But a couple of nights after his face floated up in the twilight outside the kitchen door and, swaying slightly, he invited me to drive him home. When I said How far? and he said A mile, and I started to get the car keys, my wife looked at me as if I'd taken leave of my senses. I can only say that although I had this dim sensation of being the sort of punter con men like him dream about, his very presence seemed to cast me into a light trance.

He announced (as though he'd been doing Care Work) that he'd passed the day at Taunton Races, and trying to rid myself of the 'fluence I said I hope you won. I Have Never Put A Shilling On A Horse In My Life, he said severely. He made Taunton Races sound like Taunton Assizes at which he had presided as Lord Chief Justice, and all I could come back lamely with was Why do you go, then? He answered, as though my question had led us into a world far beyond tomfools like me, To See Some Men. Going down the garden path he was full of the conditions under which he would accept what he had importuned, *viz.* How Fast Do You Drive, I Am Not Sure Your Wife Is Happy About This—even making a feint of going back into the house for her reassurance. He offered me a fag,

and when—in another weightless attempt to get my identity back into phase in the face of the man's appalling command of any ridiculous situation he might prescribe—I said No, I don't want to get cancer, he said I Will Introduce You To A Doctor.

So when I heard the gazooka I made a rude gesture, and crashed into the copse to kill the pigeons. No luck, of course, and I didn't really mind. I bore them no animus, indeed if the eating business hadn't been paramount I'd sooner have been banging away at the sort of birds who make facetious noises when a man is working in his garden. To someone sweating with exasperation as pieces of rock keep rolling out of the dry stone wall he is trying to repair, it quickly becomes apparent that the wise thrush doesn't sing each song twice over lest you should think he never could recapture the first fine careless rapture, he sings it twice because he is a dumb thrush and didn't get it right the first time.

Paranoia in the ascendant, I went deeper into the wood. And suddenly I froze. In our part of the country there are deer. There was a rustle in the boscage ahead of me—a crackling noise—a dim brown shape. My heart beat faster—if I could bring down a stag! I raised the gun, then lowered it. I wanted to be sure—supposing it was a cow?

31

Looking slightly to one side, I saw there was an open ride: if I snook out on to the path, then chucked a stone, the deer would break cover too—and I'd have him. I moved as in a dream, found a piece of rock, and heaved it.

There was a fearful noise, like the word Aaaaaargh! when you see it coming out of the mouth of someone in a cartoon, and up from the undergrowth galloped The Pill. Whether he had been snuffling for truffles I know not, but as he dashed out crying Don't shoot! I was about to lower the gun when I realised (rather like Mr. Winkle who saw the reflection of his own cowardice in the eye of Mr. Dowler) how things stood, and I put up the weapon again. With a howl, The Pill disappeared into the canebreak, and as I walked home I thought to myself I shouldn't care to eat him, casseroled or otherwise, but if that's the last we see of him, the gun's paid for itself already.

"Nonsense—we'll run for months."

32

R after EB.

NOW WE ARE PRIME MINISTER

Atticus in the Sunday Times quotes Mr. Heath's "Stepmother Mary" as saying: "He's warm, human, witty and generous. He's very considerate and never goes out without telling me where he's going; he never forgets birthdays and he rings Dad once a week . . . He does get moody sometimes . . . One night he came home in a mood and without a word he tucked Maggie May (she's one of our beagles) under his arm and went straight up to bed. He was still in a mood when he came down that morning. But that afternoon he went and bought me Thank You Very Much by the Scaffold."

Big Boy kneels at the foot of the bed.
God bless everyone. God bless Ted.
(Excuse me, God, while I kick the pup)
God bless Reggie and wake him up.
I've scrubbed my teeth—they're ever so
    clean.
Bless the Scaffold—the group, I mean.
A funny lot to remember in prayers;
I try to love them despite their hairs.
Wasn't it fun in the House tonight?
The Left so Left and the Right so Right.
(Not such fun as aboard the yacht).
Oh, God bless Harold, I quite forgot.

*

Ted Ted
(Charlemagne Prizeman)
Jolliest man alive,
Showed great
Love for his Family,
Though he was fifty-five.
Ted Ted
Said to his stepmother,
"One thing I'll never do—
I'll never take tea with the EEC
Without consulting you."

What's the matter with Teddy Heath?
He's lots of money and lots of teeth,
A racing yacht and an MBE,
So what, oh what, can the matter be?
What's the matter with moody Ted?
The beagle whimpers below his bed.
Each, in his ear, has got a flea . . .
What, oh what, can the matter be?
What's the matter with Teddy Heath?
We ought to save for a lovely wreath.
Oh, Harold has got the OBE?
Well, now we know what the matter
    could be.

*

They're changing Queens at Buckingham
    Palace—
Premier Ted goes down with Alice.
"I think the Six are terrible mean,
None of us wanted to change the Queen,"
    Says Alice.
They've sacked the Queen at Buckingham
    Palace—
Premier Ted goes down with Alice.
"Nobody wanted to change the Queen,
We just don't know where the new one's
    been . . .
And there's no more butter, just
    margarine,"
    Says Alice.

Ted has great big Mariners' boots on,
Ted has shoulders that shake and quake.
Ted has a wonderful Free French accent,
Ted (some say) is a Fake.

*

I had a penny,
A bright New Penny,
I took my penny
    On a shopping round.
You can't buy nuffin,
For Ted's left nuffin
    Under a pound.

*

I've got a string of threatened bases,
I've got experts with long, sad faces,
I know dozens of bomb-struck places—
    Who's going to sail with me?
Every morning my new grace is
Thank you, God, for a pack of aces.
Now I'm ready to sail some races—
    Who's coming out with me?

"They're incredible people! Why do they leave all this for a back street in Brixton?"

Midnight Gardener

It's lighting-up time down South, says green-fingered PETER PRESTON

Sit in the gods at the Aldwych, or any other thin cylinder of a theatre, on first nights and there far below as the final act ends a dozen little lights weave around in the stalls. A myriad of grumpy glow-worms. The critics with their famed critical pens—ballpoints with a fitted bulb. He who lives in the dark slays in the dark. One new Tynan showed me his electronic implementa the other day, a pushbutton pass to true professionalism. "Who'd think such Popean fury could flow from a trumped-up torch?" he said. I found it a bit lunatic. There is something inane about big men from El Vino's groping through gloom; something other-worldly about miners in their headgear; and something definitively dotty about General Electric's latest (American) lawn mower.

To explain: from a Northwest Orient or somesuch Boeing over suburban America at night, the dusky canvas looks strangely akin to the orchestra stalls. Thin ribbons of motorama; flashing hamburger joints; back-porch barbecues broiling spare ribs for spare people; and the GE mower, freshest of the fresh, puttering up and down sprawling lawns, a twinkle of futility.

The market research notion is that Americans today have too scanty light-time for gardening. They want to drive home from the office, take a couple of highballs, sup, and then dig. By which time it's dark. By which route come General Electric, with their headlamp-fitted mower. Nicely suppressed, so the colour TV next door survives without interference. Painstakingly silenced, so those who sleep early may sleep undisturbed. Place orders now for full floodlighting to make your garden a midnight sunspot; or, alternatively, this luminous trowel comes somewhat cheaper.

Obviously, various researchers have various explanations for the bizarre demand. Gardening is healthy, a recreational rocket replacing unalloyed television. Gardening represents Father America yearning to cast off mechanical coils and play simple Johnny Appleseed again. Back to nature and back to bunkum. Several of my closest acquaintances are ferocious gardeners, and only one trait links their passion: none of them can stand his wife for long stretches. Each morning on the way to work I pass a minute semi whose resident man can, with utter predictability, be found on his pocket handkerchief lawn, trimming it a blade at a time. On the way back from work there's no such retreat for him and from the front parlour booms inevitable Belfastian belligerence, the din of domestic disruption. QED. You can garden near somebody. You can't garden with them. What better escape from strife than a relaxing nocturnal spin on the mower? Can it Sadie or I'll dump the cuttings in your goddamn poolside patio.

A blessedly solitary pursuit, then; but so is lying in bed with the curtains drawn and the door locked. What sets gardening aside is that it's essentially non-enjoyable fun. It's a modern leisure sector, the unpleasantness integral, necessary, indispensable. You do it because you have to be alone; but you wouldn't do it if it wasn't thoroughly miserable to boot.

Consider the great gardens of England, repositories of stately tradition, pastures in which the lovable yokel Fred Streeter once toiled. They give intense enjoyment to the beholder, but hardly to the toiler. Is any area of British unionism more individually morose than the sons of the soil? Absolutely not: tap a farmworker about his woes and the flood of fury exceeds a Dagenham fitter or Merthyr miner. And pro gardeners are just the

"Good Lord—is it the end of the financial year already?"

same. Does a golden-haired child stray among their geraniums? The foul bellow rises. Does an astigmatic Alsatian foul their greensward? Small sniffy signs threaten small sniffy fines. They are a tetchy, rheumy, underpaid, over-soaked society. They know gardening isn't much of a life. They do it for life. They have always done it for those who could afford to pay. Only within two decades of affluence (plus proliferating commercial gear and thus advertising) has the hoe become a symbol of success—success in earning enough to have soil rather than concrete at your back window, success in having the time to potter among the primroses.

The solitariness is crucial: compare gardening with housework, for instance, which can be done in packs and has never acquired a breath of social cachet. But the aura of sweaty distaste is just as vital. Leisure minus pleasure. A mandatory hobby. A non-rest cure which tells us a good deal about evolving American (and other) society.

Sociologists without number have addressed themselves to the problem of shorter working weeks and greater family boredom. Four days out of seven shall ye lightly labour, and then what? Sit in a chair and watch Miss World? On the contrary, the proffered relaxations are merely fresh unpaid work disguised as a swan. If you must play a game, play golf, which in its passionate neuroses and ultimate futilities captures the essence of boardroom politicking. Nobody enjoys golf. Every middle-aged player I know returns from his round shagged and morose, all set to sleep the evening away in precisely the style he contrives after a tough day's office. Fishing is

"This Sunday I intend to talk about the seriousness of the population explosion."

"There must be some misunderstanding, the three and a half million was just for the model."

exactly the same. A long, dour hike to a dismal stream; a drenching wrestle; a pathetic token of a trout to appease the wife for absence. Did you enjoy it, dear? Naturally not, but it did me good.

Our expanding leisure areas are, in short, being gradually converted into expanding grindstones. The full-time housewife whom I meet who writes, and Open Universities "for fun," is far more flaked at the end of the day than any lady journalist extant. The sandwich coursers and the Shelter helpers and the coffee morners. Our empty existences filled with bits and pieces which do little good but cloak their vapidity in vague social usefulness. My Continental friends roaming the French provinces report a substantial change in Gallic time-wasting. Only a few years ago it was football on the table, the whirling handles and Pernod game. Now every spare corner boasts a machine to "test your reflexes." Put a coin in at the top and try and block it before it falls to the bottom. No more absorbing than table football; indeed, a large measure less diverting. But educational because quasi-scientific. Not a waste of effort, Gaston. Even the business of concocting an intellectual front grows harder. I once had a very enjoyable ferret round George Formby's library full of the most amazing books that he bought by the yard. Now comedians buy sets of Charles Dickens at twelve pounds a time from "stupendous classics of the month" clubs.

The tale of those beaming, muffled little mowers in their sulking American gardens is, in sum, a tale of pathetic delirium. Herman's life before he reaches for the rake and hurricane lamp isn't exceeding endeavour, but filling the flabby hour. His light on the lawn alerts neighbours to industry, shuts out domesticity with its circle. Parkinson, you should be hedge-trimming at this hour: except that the unhappy Professor, outstripped by events, is having to write another book to keep himself in business.

On the off-chance it might meet up with aliens out in space, Pioneer 10, the first-ever spacecraft to leave our solar system, carries this simple greetings card . . .

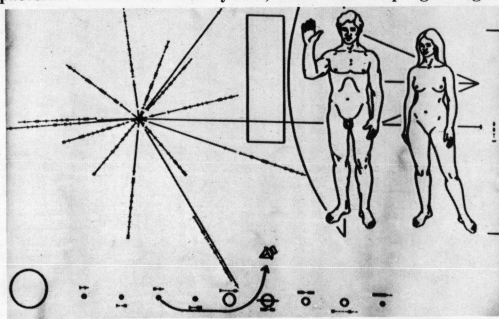

But according to the *Herald Tribune*, only one in ten of NASA scientists was able to figure out its message. So what chance have the aliens got?

"Us aliens," remarked an alien intelligence, "are forever getting this sort of thing coming winging at us unsolicited out of the skies and, quite frankly, it's a job to know what the half of it means. Whoever sent this latest one clearly doesn't appreciate that out there somewhere, amongst the billions and billions of tiny white specks, there must be dozens of little worlds peopled by mad, compulsive doodlers, sending this sort of trash out willy-nilly into the ether. Yet they never think to put a postmark on, no name and address, not even a flag. They must think everybody up here is a super-omniscient mekon of some sort, but there's still an awful lot of us who have got better things to do than look at cryptic diagrams out of the blue.

"This latest arrival is a rum one and no mistake. Clearly, it's a circus of some kind. As far as we can make out, it seems to depict a comical turn by a fourteen-legged and uncommonly thin spider which is using a block of wood to knock a toadstool on its side. Or it might be one of those things which certain organisms use for squeezing oranges on. It's hard to say with those two creatures standing in the way, or perhaps they are advanced vegetables. Either way, one seems to be telling this thin spider to desist. Or then again, perhaps that it's got five more tries.

"Still, I must emphasise that we are only guessing at this stage and none of us has been able to explain the significance of the dots along the bottom. A suggestion that it could be a map of some metropolitan railway has been made to us, but we feel that this fails to take into account the arrowed position of a capsized yacht, or possibly a garden trowel. The inclusion of a naked blonde makes it more than likely, however, that this is some kind of a joke sent out by a backward planet, possibly that being used by the Earthlings."

———

"Speaking as a fourteen-legged and extremely thin spider," said a voice from the back of Andromeda 9, "I have studied this post-card from the Earthlings and I take it as a snub. The caricature of our species is both crude and inept, suggesting, amongst other things, that we've got a right leg longer than all the rest. Furthermore, the geometric being which is standing at the back has clearly turned its back on us and one of the other two is pointing five antennae in a frankly sordid gesture. There seems little reason to doubt, amongst us intelligent spiders, that this thing is intended as a declaration of war. The illustrated talent for the creature on the right to be capable of firing arrows from the shoulder is a particularly sinister turn and one that bodes badly for a long and bitter struggle with the Earthlings."

"Whatever it is," the Being declared, "it's not come all this way for nothing. My guess is that it's trying to tell us something. Just suppose, for argument's sake, that this thing which we have before us is not an actual creature itself but an artefact of some sort. Such a theory might explain for a start why it hasn't so far uttered in any way. No, this thing was sent — probably from some primitive three-dimensional world—and I say it's meant to be a picture or a cipher with a message for us Beings. What the message is, of course, depends on which way up it's supposed to be. I shouldn't be a bit surprised if it was rude."

———

"Magnificent!" The thing on Alpha Centaurus was overcome with awe. "Truly magnificent! As far as is known this is the first time ever that has fetched up on our planet an original work by the erstwhile Earthling Leonardo da Vinci. Our telescopes show that the style is unmistakably his. Nevertheless, the discovery is bound to alter some of intelligence data on the Earth. It was not known until now, that the climate was sufficiently warm for policemen to go on point duty without clothes in their world nor that key limbs on the Earthlings are apparently operated by string. Let us hope they send us further simple greetings-cards soon."

When the Role is Called up Yonder

Liverpudlian GILLIAN REYNOLDS prepares
to act out a few Southern fantasies

I am ninety-eight per cent sure, and that's surer than most people are born these days, that about this time of year a little man stations himself on the right hand side of the Great Concourse at Euston station and passes out cards to likely looking travellers with the message inscribed thereupon,

"When in Liverpool
      Drop in on the Reynolds."

Of course the message might be a bit different. It might say, judging from the people who've been dropping in on us over Christmas for the past ten years,

"Ale for dogs
      Chez Stan."

This last being the sort of idiomatic and esoteric message likely to appeal to returning Liverpudlians since the correct interpretation of it is only a variant reading of the equally ancient rune

"Jars Out
      At Gill's."

Liverpool, as I'm sure the rest of the country knows only too well by now, is to the exiled Liverpudlian as the spawning ground is to the salmon. It must be returned to, and if the returning cannot be done in person then God help the exile's audience as they sit through the night petrified with boredom at the never ending flow of folk tales about the night Docker Doyle got barred out of the Blue Angel, the Christmas Me Auntie Mary caught her drawers in the hinge of the seat of the outside lav, or the Boxing Day Sheila Kelly, age of nine, pinched the port and gave herself the nosebleed while doing the high kicks.

People used to come home for the Grand National and elections too but that was mostly in the 'fifties when the world took that kind of thing seriously. Nowadays the exiles return en masse only for Christmas. They step onto the train at Euston, their hands full of gift wrapped bundles and their hearts aglow with a vision of Christmas in Liverpool dancing before their inner eye. Seen as if through a frost rimmed window pane, lit by the flame from a red candle held by an angelic choirboy with a surplice on him that looks like it's been made from a paper doily, the exile's vision makes Christmas at home full of the magic of the *Chick's Own Annual* (remember *Chick's Own*—the com-ic that split up diff-i-cult words so that ti-ny rea-ders could manage them?) and mam's cooking, with the promise of a week on the ale with The Old Fella and Our Kid.

For two hours and forty minutes the returning exile will unlock his word hoard to capture this vision for the rest of the occupants of his compartment as the train sweeps through Rugby,

"A gentleman here says he might be interested in the salvage rights, sir."

Stafford, Crewe and finally Runcorn, for once over the Runcorn Bridge the exile is home, craning out of the window to catch a look at Fords on the left, Goodlass Wall on the right, St. Anthony of Padua's on one side, Wavertree Playground (known to all genuine Liverpudlians as The Mystery, though why is another mystery) till the train pulls through the tunnel just past Edge Hill and finishes on Platform 7 at Lime Street. Then what a bursting of carriage doors there is, what a stumbling out (courtesy of Messrs. Guinness and the able buffet staff of British Rail), what a sniffing of the sea moist air, what a hailing of porters who have flown helter skelter into dark corners at the sight of struggling passengers, what a waiting for taxis ("Where you going, chief? I'm not taking fares outside the North End.")

In all its fascination the city lies before them, concrete, muck and sick filled gutters, lit by the blaze from a thousand headlamps of motor cars

stalled by a traffic jam in the Tunnel. Soon he is home, or is he? If he does return to the ancestral bosom the exile is received with tears and suspicious looks. ("Are you out of work, just when I thought you were nicely settled.") The advanced exile takes, therefore, a room at the best hotel in town, descends to the bar for a drink and is greeted by the barman, "I thought we'd seen the last of you after the fight on New Year's Day." The latter category of exile (usually they write plays) also notices the conversation stops when they are near mainly because the talkers have discovered they tend to turn up lightly fictionalised on the telly six months after. It is at this moment that the exile's hand strays to the slip of pasteboard in his pocket, the one the little man at Euston pressed upon him.

Twenty minutes later he finds himself on our doorstep, cursing as he plunges his hand through the holly wreath to reach the knocker. Once the door opens his real troubles begin. He probably thought he knew us but when he sees us face to face it usually turns out it was Our Billy's friend Jane he knew, and not very well at that. Never mind, it's lovely to see someone from London. Come on in, you'll never guess who's here. There's Billy and Valerie (he's the one with mohair suit and she's the one with the makeup), you must know them, they live in Clapham. You remember Paul, he had a record reached 17 last April, or was it the April before?

Now I must make perfectly plain here that all my guests invited, uninvited and drift-ins, are welcome. There is nothing I like more than being the hostess, posing around in the long dress and offering people baked meats. I am the one the cookery editors reach when they print all those recipes for seventy-two ways with leftover turkey, I am a sucker for prescriptions for punch, instructions for fashioning angels from rolls of kitchen foil, notions for nibblers and the myriad tips on graciousness which fly from all directions at this time of the year. I must admit, too, that it's hard going. I wouldn't say I'm the world's worst cook, that would give me some kind of rarity value but I will admit that when our festive board groans, it's usually passing an opinion. Nevertheless, I try. I school the children to walk round with trays of canapes and offer views on Tolkien. I leave around copies of "Rolling Stone" and "IT." I've even been known to persuade my husband to fetch the coal in while there are strangers in the house.

In short, I consider it a duty to keep our end up, to make it plain to visiting Londoners that there's a whole big world of civilisation up there beyond Watford. We know what Campari is, all right, and we know a dish of crudites when we see one, too. Don't think it's going to be all scouse and bottles of brown ale when you come to our house. We're in touch, we have a postal subscription to the "Evening Standard."

Yet the evidence of my experience shows that this is just what the visiting exile does not want. He can get all that avocado pear stuff back in The Smoke. What he wants when he gets back home to The 'Pool is the scruffy fun of yesteryear. The brawling on the pavements, the spewing in the halls, the disgusting food made from the wrong end of an old ewe's ribs, foaming pints of bitter in glasses shaped like flower pots, aunties that cry after two sherries (British) and kids who fall asleep under the pile of coats on the sofa. Who needs all the Sunday supplement graciousness when they're only home for the holiday week?

Ever ready to oblige and constantly determined to keep up with market trends, this year I am

approaching the Festive Season more suitably. The children will be referred to by their hereditary Liverpool titles of The Lad, The Little Fellow, and The Baby. Dinner will be what you eat in the afternoon, pots of tea will be served with all food. Custard, thick and yellow and lumpy just like Gran used to make, will be poured over all puddings. Salt fish will be boiled on Christmas Eve so that the hallways will be filled with the aroma of long forgotten childhood. The intervals between eating and dish washing will be filled with "turns," that is, everyone will be called upon to do a song, dance, recitation or impersonation, and the best "turn" will oblige with the Jim Reeves medley. Guests arriving in pairs must be accompanied by a crate of ale. Guests with small, scuttling, screaming, underfoot children will be especially welcome. If it's the traditional, olde tyme, Merseyside Yule that's wanted, then that's what we'll be serving up this year, cinders, fog, finnan haddie and all. After all, it's better to be dead of indigestion than out of fashion.

*"Now **that's** impressive!"*

"Why, Mrs. Wainwright!—You shouldn't have."

"Bouncer!"

For all those women readers who felt cheated by our recent parody of the magazine for men, McMURTRY bids you welcome to the delights of the

PLAYGIRL CLUB

"Tis a walkover, lads—part-time three nights a week and already Oi'm Bunny of the Month."

"Don't forget, Albert lad—if that Sue Heffer starts anything, use my hatpin!"

"Please Dad!—You promised!"

I'll Never Forgive What's His Name

GEORGE MIKES has always hated him but forgets for the minute why.

Should I hate Hirohito, Emperor of Japan, formerly Sun-God but recently promoted human, or should I love him with warmth and devotion? I am afraid our excellent newspapers and periodicals offered me very limited and often confusing advice on this issue. And I needed advice badly because I am one of the worst haters alive.

Sometimes I get extremely angry with someone and decide never to speak to him—or his wife and all descendants—again. Then, after a while, I meet him unexpectedly and having forgotten my grievance, I embrace him and kiss him on both cheeks. Or else, I may remember vaguely that I ought to hate this fellow for some very good reason but, for the life of me, cannot remember why. I try to make an effort to recall the incident but how on earth can I hate him when, really, I quite like him? And even, in the rare cases, when I do remember his crime, it always looks so petty and trivial after the lapse of some time.

It is the same with some great wars, recorded in history and taught at school. Was it really worth while to shed so much blood in the War of Austrian Succession? Was it so important to a poor Andalusian peasant whether the Pragmatic Sanction was valid and whether Philip V, King of Spain, should occupy the throne of Austria, or August III of Saxony or Maria Theresa should go on ruling as if she were a male. I am glad Maria Theresa won but not all *that* glad. And was it really of any consequence how the spoils of the First Balkan War were distributed when subsequent Balkan Wars redistributed the spoils all over again, in any case? And if great dynastic and religious wars sink into triviality, how much less important it seems whether my friend did or did not cheat me to the tune of £85,000? What is £85,000 between friends? And why should A resent that B has slept with his wife when C, D, E, F, G, H, J, K, L and M have also slept with her. Why pick on B?

An absolute beginner though I may be as a hater, I am ready—indeed, eager—to learn. Whom to hate? Why? How intensely? How long? And when exactly to stop?

Let me make one thing clear as far as Emperor Hirohito and the Japanese are concerned. I accept and bow to the feelings of anyone who was a prisoner in their hands during the last war. Who are we, who never experienced those horrors, to give a lesson and offer guidance to those who did? But even they puzzle me occasionally. Some of them—Russell Braddon, the writer, for example, who suffered tremendously in those camps, advises us most generously to bury the hatchet and forgive. Others, however, say that while it was all right to invite the Emperor, it was utterly wrong to give him (or rather give him *back*) the Order of the Garter. To me the exact opposite would seem logical: send him the Most Noble Order of the Garter by post; add the Thistle, the Bath, the Royal Order of Victoria and Albert, throw in an OBE—but tell him to keep away. Then, why hate the *Japanese*? Why not the Fascists? The militarists? The totalitarians? The aggressors? The imperialists? Why go on hating the people who operated the Burma camps but love those who ran Auschwitz? What about the former Vichyites? The murderers at Katyn?

And it is here where some of my strong convictions come into play. I *am* a bad hater but I have strong principles, and some of them make me hesitate to join the Common Market, fervently though I may support the idea otherwise. I have many French friends and love them dearly as individuals but I shall never—never!—forgive the French their intrigues to alienate Aquitaine—our lawful possession—in 1334. And even if I were ready to sweep the painful memories of the Hundred Years War under the carpet (as I am not), how can I forgive Napoleon Bonaparte? Not so much his aggression (that was second nature to him) but he made some really nasty and malicious remarks about us English, which I shall never condone. And how can I associate with the Germans when the Kaiser was decidedly unfriendly and unkind to his own cousin and not too nice to Queen Victoria, his grandmother? What can we expect from modern Germans who are not even our grandchildren?

A lot of people think that the Italians are better. In fact, they are worse. They are the descendants of the Romans. You may forgive Julius Caesar's invasion of Britain but I am not as easy-going in serious matters; and you may think that they treated Boadicea chivalrously but I violently disagree with you. I do not want to go into long details about my objections to associating with the Belgians and the Dutch (those differences concerning the right of search at sea still rancour) but with Luxembourg I refuse to play ball. I have a strong suspicion that they had a leading role in the establishment of the Dutch East India Company in rivalry with us and that, I am afraid, is too much for me.

". . . and now we come to the Dry Martini Ceremony."

The People, that voice of wisdom and intellect, thinks differently. They discard these outdated and worthless notions of nationalism and divide the world into two halves: young 'uns and old 'uns. Young Japanese are good; old Japanese are bad. Guilty fathers versus innocent sons. Some low-type characters may insinuate that this is an attempt by middle-aged squares to ingratiate themselves with youth but anyone who knows *The People* would reject such a suggestion with scorn. They declare that "our young people know perfectly well" (mind you, the young know it; the old do not but they do not count in any case) "that young Japan is ashamed of those past horrors." I—one of the old ones, I must admit—know nothing of all this. I was given the strong impression in Japan that the whole nation—old ones as well as young—remember only too well that they were the only live targets for nuclear weapons and are ready—most generously—to forgive us for *our* brutality and inhumanity which dwarfs theirs. But "being ashamed"? Oh no. In any case, *The People,* as always, is right. Hate the old Japanese and love the young Japanese. That reduces the target of your hatred by about 65 per cent and the less people you hate the better.

But is it? Isn't the clue to this whole hatred business the melancholy fact that we *need* hatred? As an internal combusion engine needs to get rid of poisonous gas, so the human psyche needs exactly the same. Love is our noblest emotion but love cannot exist without hate—just as goodness becomes meaningless without viciousness, beauty without ugliness. It does not really matter whom you hate as long as you hate someone. You may hate old Japanese; others young Turks; again others middle-aged Finns. The object is immaterial; hatred itself is a blessing and a necessity.

You should, really, love yourself. It is not always easy but you must try. I am not madly keen on myself but I got used to living with myself. I accept myself with a sigh of resignation and—after all these years of co-habitation—I grew rather fond of myself. Admittedly, I could improve; but I could be much, much worse. Only people who love themselves are capable of loving others. But from this it follows—all feelings being ambivalent—that only people who also hate themselves will be able to love others; and only people who hate at least some will be able to love the rest. So one of the noblest doctrines I can pass down to posterity is this: Hate Thy Neighbour as Thou Hatest Thyself. But, on second thoughts, why your neighbour? Love your neighbour and hate old Japanese. And Japanese, in turn, should love *their* neighbours and hate old Yorkshiremen. And Outer Mongolians should love their neighbours and hate middle-aged Tanzanians. But we should all love *The People* for pointing humanity's way to a happier and brighter future.

"I got that one for walking through Soho without stopping."

45

"It's Father Rooney, men, he's come to bless the petrol."

The I.R.A.

*A week in the life of the Chosen Few
by MAHOOD*

"Paddy tells me you want to abide by the Geneva Convention. You're a
disgrace to the uniform, O'Toole!"

"It's too damn quiet for my liking—they must be holding another press conference."

"And now for the eyesight test—how many bullets could you put in his back from twenty-five yards?"

"Can I have the gun tonight, Da?"

"Jasus Sean! You can't go out to murder people dressed like that!"

"Just because we shot a few soldiers without benefit of trial doesn't give them the right to intern us without benefit of trial."

Flowers and vegetables have highly developed, almost human, e
plants with a polygraph. Cabbages "faint" before being boiled.

from
THE GUARDIAN

Rape (writes Jill Tweedie) is not a thing you come across every day. A pity, because when approached with an open mind it can be quite rewarding and even memorable. The trouble is that nobody has ever bothered to publicise it much; as a result, its image is dull, stuffy and sometimes objectionable, which means that many people who would enjoy rape opt for something they think is more exciting, and miss out on an experience that may not be world-shattering but is worth trying once.

The best way to cook this unassuming green vegetable (cont. p. 94)

from the Times Literary Supplement
A CLOCKWORK ORANGE
by Anthony Burgess

Another delightful children's story from Mr. Burgess, this time about Oliver Orange and his visit to London. While there he is set upon by a gang of nasty greengages who leave him cut and leaking in the gutter, but he is befriended by kindly Dr. Banana who fits him out with a tiny clockwork motor! Well again, he and the doctor have a series of exciting adventures (including a visit in a fruit basket to Buckingham Palace) but eventually Oliver has to go back to his native Seville.

from
THE TIMES
Personal Column

HOME WANTED for two young geraniums, sensitive, used to fairly intelligent conversations. Applications, with references, to Box H40.

THOUSANDS of cotton plants are murdered every day so that we can wear shirts. Help oppose this bloody trade by giving to the Anti-Vivisection Fund.

AN ELDERLY apple tree in Battersea had not been sprayed or pruned for five years. If we had not come to his aid, he would now be in a very bad way. Please send your contribution to the Distressed Fruit Tree Association.

LARGE GARDEN in Italy to rent, from May. Many friendly roses, serious-minded chrysanthemums etc. Have a gardening holiday this year—beginners welcomed. Call Supermulch Vacations.

WHEN YOUR loved one departs, spare a thought for our dumb friends. Say "No flowers by request". Floral Defence League.

YOUNG MAN grow anywhere, dig anything. Box 385.

from
THE BALD
CAULIFLOWER
by DESMOND MORRIS

Now that we know that man is descended, via animals, from a vanished form of aggressive, gregarious spinach, we can make a much more informed guess at the mystery of human hair. Why is there so much variety? Why does an Afro-frizzy cut seem beautiful in New York and long blonde hair in Sweden? The answer lies in the group-unconscious memory of the arrival of the cauliflower. When our ancestors were still rooted in some primeval kitchen garden, all green, all contented to be a lettuce or a cabbage, the arrival of the cauliflower must have had a cataclysmic effect. This sexually proud, territorially demanding, ornament-conscious plant, with its huge arrogant white knob, can only have sown discord in those far-off seed beds. Our urge today to arrange the top of our heads into pleasing, attractive patterns, is, though we may not realise it, an attempt to compete with the cauliflower.

(Next week: Onions and why we cry.)

responses, concludes a New York researcher after six years testing

s are nervous in the presence of dogs. Where do we go from here?

PLANTED FREE

by JOY ADAMSON

This is the heart-warming story of two baby Flesh-Eating Lilies that Joy Adamson found uprooted one day in the jungle and took into her home to nurture. There, Attila and Genghis — as they came to be known—quickly recovered, and thanks to Joy's care and devotion managed to lead a happy life as seedlings, playing for hours with a lamb chop or mischievously nipping the Adamsons' puppy. Mrs. Adamson has some fascinating things to say about the psychology of carnivorous lilies, which are absolutely fearless, somewhat flippant yet devoted friends. Sadly, the day came when Attila and Genghis took a large chunk out of Joy's little finger, and they reluctantly decided it was time to let them go free. They were planted out in the jungle some miles away, but the Adamsons know, by the occasional scream of a small mouse, that they are still alive and hunting. (The paper used for the book comes from swiftly and painlessly felled trees.)

from the

GOOD FOOD GUIDE

FAD'S   Sloane Street, S.W.1.

Ernest and Sidney are two ex-vegetarians who ran Greenery in the King's Road till they discovered the anguish and misery caused by killing fruit and vegetables. Now, at Fad's, they offer only food which can be prepared without involving pain. Among their more unusual dishes are Monosodium Glutamate in Vitamin D sauce (70p), Brewer's Yeast a la Greque (65p) and Sea Crystal Cocktail (40p), while our inspector had a very good Chlorophyll Soup (40p). The main complaints seem to centre on the desserts, with Artificial Colouring Pudding coming in for a lot of criticism. There is a quite interesting water list.
C1. Shamrock and Poppy Day.
Meals, 12-3, 6-10. No dogs or locusts.
App. Yehudi Menuhin; Jonathan Miller; the editor of The Ecologist; John Lennon.

STOP
THIS CRUELTY NOW!

Every year thousands of visitors to Wales are shocked and horrified by their first encounter with the national sport, leek-fighting. In 'guest-houses' throughout the country they are brought face to face with the leek (which has already been weakened by several hours in boiling water) and given a knife and fork to deal with it. A highly skilled performer can finish it off in a few minutes, but all too often the leek slips sodden off the fork, bursts under the impact of the knife or simply dissolves, postponing the senseless slaughter for hours. Frequently, its carcase is just pushed to the side of the plate and abandoned. The Welsh call it a great tradition. They talk of the symbolism of man's eternal battle against the vegetable. They point out that the fighter is armed only with a knife and fork, that he could easily slip and cut himself. They declare that the leek enjoys the struggle. They insist on the gay pageantry involving aprons, dropping fag-ends and bits of soil.
This is all sophistry. Leek-fighting is barbaric and immoral.
It must be banned now !

Issued by the RSPCV

to the editor of

THE TIMES

Sir,
In Fortnum's yesterday (Feb 22) we distinctly saw the first spring onion.

yours etc
KENNETH TYNAN
ARNOLD WESKER
etc

On a Distant Prospect of Eton College

Sophia Loren has declared her intention of sending her son to Eton. She has, of course, tried a number of other public schools, too : with little success as yet . . .

During recent preparations of the cricket pitch for the coming season, James Nold, 47, a Winchester groundsman, was startled when a half-clad lady sprang aboard his mower and began shrieking about her son's amazing grasp of trigonometry. "Her suddenly appeared at deep fine leg," he said, "and afore I knew it, she'm grabbed my handbrake. I tole her I weren't the Headmaster soon as I got a word in edgeways, and she screamed summat foreign and ran orf."

A misguided attempt by Miss Loren to influence the headmaster of St. Ignatius's Jesuit Seminary. Arriving at the gates, she informed the porter that she wished to discuss her son's future, and he set the dogs on her. He has subsequently become a Muslim.

An unhappy moment at Marlborough Military Academy. The headmaster, who lost his right ear in the Western Desert, has just discovered that Miss Loren's sister is Mussolini's daughter-in-law.

A heartbroken Stowe housemaster explains to Miss Loren that her son's application form arrived too late.

An unfortunate incident at the Gordonstoun Open Day. Miss Loren, hoping for a word with the Bursar, strolled casually onto the field during the Fathers Hundred Yards Dash. It was won in 9.2 seconds, and seventy-eight of the contestants were treated in hospital for cuts, bruises, shock, and lust.

****** and the Law**

FENTON BRESLER
sums up on
o*sc*n* l*ng**g*

I never thought I would feel sorry for Germaine Greer. But now, amazingly, the day has arrived. For the poor darling has been fined £17 in an Auckland magistrates' court for using what the newspapers euphemistically call "a four-letter word" in a lecture at Auckland University. Her vocabulary must have been quite considerably curtailed.

Such a monstrous restriction on the right of free speech could never have occurred in England. Ever since the Divisional Court quashed a conviction for "indecent language" against Alan Ginsberg for reading aloud to some two hundred people on Brighton sea-front one of his poems with the epic line: "Go ---- yourself with the atom bomb", obscenities in the cause of the arts or higher education have been perfectly legal. That was in the summer of 1968; and ever since a hundred flowers have bloomed.

In films, in plays, on television, even in the occasional late-night radio show many a powerful four- to eight-letter word has triumphed. As a spokesman for the Law Society commented last June about that most awful four-letter word of all beginning with 'F': "It is used on the stage and in responsible publications. The law should reflect current thinking."

Quite so. Miss Greer's use of only a marginally less horrendous word was, after all, during a lecture. It is unthinkable that any English judge or magistrate would have convicted her.

Indeed, it is now the law that not only actors and academics can be foulmouthed. Early last year, a London policeman stopped a Walthamstow

*"The Crown against O'Grady. D'you call **that** Justice?"*

motor fitter because he suspected he might be carrying stolen goods in his van. The motor fitter suggested that the policeman was making a fuss about nothing and inquired "forcefully" about his legal right to search his van. During this inquiry, that most awful four-letter word of all was used.

Dismissing a charge brought under the 1839 Metropolitan Police Act of using obscene language to the annoyance of passers-by, stipendiary magistrate Mr. Ian McLeod commented in a worldly fashion: "It is an adjective used by some people who know no other. Is it really obscene in 1971?" Obviously, the learned magistrate did not think so, and he does not seem to have worried whether the policeman agreed with him or not. I suppose he thought the police are case-hardened to this kind of abuse. They are past being "annoyed" by it. The acquitted motor fitter was delighted. "I feel the magistrate was right to find me not guilty," he said afterwards. "You hear the word on television and in films. I have heard women use far worse."

Indeed, so has the Rev. Harry Dawson, 44-year old father of two who is minister of Elim Pentecostal Church in East Ham, London. In his parish newsletter last May, Mr. Dawson protested about the way local housewives damned and blasted their way through the High Street.

"For myself," said Mr. Dawson, "if I hit my thumb I say 'Praise the Lord'. I think that's much better." But in the shops he heard the whole range of swear words from women. And they didn't even swear in a soft, ladylike way. "They use the words loudly and in quite ordinary conversation," complained Mr. Dawson.

Naturally, these days, no one was arrested or charged with a criminal offence. Unlike the three Punjabis in Bradford, Yorkshire, who had darned bad luck a couple of years ago. They were swearing fluently at each other in Punjabi on top of a bus—unfortunately, within ear-shot of the only Punjabi-speaking policeman in England. It cost them each a £3 fine.

In the old days, the law was clear. The 1745 Profane Oaths Act laid down a specific tariff for swearing—and it made no difference whether you did it in private or in public. Rather like consenting male adults before the Wolfenden law reform—either way, it was illegal.

Section 1 of the 1745 Act proclaimed it an offence for "any person profanely to curse or swear". And the penalty was, as follows:

For a day labourer, or common soldier, sailor or seaman—1s.

For any other person under the degree of a gentleman—2s.

For every person of or above the degree of a gentleman—5s.

And for a second offence, in whatever category, the penalty was doubled. For a third offence, it was trebled.

"*Now come along, children. It's time to dial-a-prayer and then off to bed with you.*"

"*Lock your doors, shutter your windows—the McCluskey brothers are riding into town.*"

"*Women and children off the streets, the McCluskey brothers are riding into town.*"

It will be noted that "women" or "ladies" are not specifically referred to. And the better legal view, as stated in *Stone's Justices' Manual* that adorns every magistrates' clerk's desk in the land, was that the Act "does not appear to apply to women, and the words seem to be repugnant to their being included."

Germaine Greer and the modern liberated woman would have had nothing to fear from this piece of repressive guilt-ridden legislation—even though it continued in full force until as recently as 1967 when the Labour Government, in a typical flourish of "permissive society" decadence, repealed the entire Act.

The supporters of Harold Wilson's repealing statute would presumably have agreed with Mia Farrow, the well-known actress and mother of twins, who in Bow Street magistrates' court one cold November day in 1968 somewhat startled the packed courtroom by proclaiming happily from the witness box: "If you say - - - -, that is the nicest thing you can wish anybody." I suppose it's a point of view. Mr. Kenneth Harington, the Bow Street magistrate, "remained unmoved", one newspaper reporter assured us. After all, what could he say? Both to deny or agree with the sentiment could have been embarrassing.

"*Take to the hills, the McCluskey brothers are riding into town.*"

Yet there is a limit to all this marvellous freedom and liberty of expression. Earlier this year, last month in fact, the Divisional Court ruled that that most awful four-letter word of all *could* still be obscene.

Yet another London motorist had used the word no less than six times to express his opinion of a policeman on traffic duty—including telling him that he must be "- - - -ing blind." The Willesden magistrate threw out a charge of usuing obscene language to the annoyance of passers-by: they said they were not sure that "in this day and age" anyone would be shocked.

But the police appealed—and they won. The magistrates had overlooked a vital piece of evidence that two women thought the motorist's outburst was "shocking". That did it! The Divisional Court ruled that it was not open for the magistrates to say they were not sure that anyone would nowadays be shocked or annoyed by such an expression. The fact remains that these two women had been—and that was enough to merit a conviction.

Beauty may well be in the eye of the beholder. But obscenity is also in the ear of the listener.

If an old lady was shocked by the language she heard at a modern play or one of the more sophisticated London theatres, the actor or actress could still today be charged with a criminal offence. But I should think they are fairly safe. Aunt Edna does not go to that sort of play or theatre anyway.

"*Nice quiet town brother.*"

Superkid By WILLIAM DAVIS

The *Daily Telegraph,* a reader of that esteemed journal suggested the other day, "is infinitely more harmful" to school-children than *Oz.* It is a point worth debating: if the argument is to be about what corrupts children (and if it isn't, the whole business is really too tedious for words) then we really ought not to confine ourselves to obscenity.

Is the *Telegraph* harmful? I suppose one could argue that its extensive reports of the *Oz* trial, and the aftermath, corrupted many more children than the original issue could ever hope to do. It whetted appetites that should have stayed unwhetted. But let's not talk about sex—or, if we must, let us reflect, in passing, that the *Sun* and *News of the World,* whose distribution to wholesome British homes is somewhat larger than that of *Oz* or *Ink,* have more influence in that department than a whole army of Richard Nevilles.

Where the *Telegraph* could be said to exercise a harmful influence is in its stout defence of Establishment virtues—its class-consciousness, its admiration of conformity, its impatience with anyone who dares to challenge established concepts.

But let us not be nasty to what is, without doubt, a great newspaper. Let us agree that there are many ways of corrupting young minds—that racial intolerance, blind chauvinism, the glorification of war, and arrogance based on nothing more than an accident of birth are, in their way, no less objectionable than smut. Let us agree, too, that it makes a change to talk about the power of the printed word (or drawing) rather than about the menace of TV.

Whatever the majority of children read, it certainly isn't *Oz* or *Ink.* What do they buy, and what influence, if any, does it have on them?

The answer, of course, depends on the age group to which they belong. At five, it's still likely to be Three Blind Mice and Fee Fi Fo Fum. (I was also brought up on the Brothers Grimm and Wilhelm Busch—both every bit as liable to currupt as Disney.) After that, to the age of fourteen and often beyond, children tend to be hung up on comics. Older boys and girls read magazines like *Honey, Petticoat,* and *Romance.* And, of course, all of them pick up the publications brought home by their parents—including *Punch.*

The voluminous correspondence produced by the *Oz* verdict made me curious about the propaganda line taken by the schoolkids' press. So I

54

started by reading through eighteen different comics published last week. My first reaction was one of astonishment at how little they have changed over the years. Do children really still say gosh, crumbs, and golly? Do they talk about "pesky hounds" and use phrases like "Oh, you rotter?" The comics say they do: Billy Bunter, still going strong in *Valiant and Smash*, hasn't got a day older. The villains, too, seem much the same: swots, know-alls, and tell-tales still get into awful trouble.

There is, Judge Argyle will be relieved to hear, no sex in British comics. None whatever. As far as the publishers are concerned, it simply does not exist. American comics tend to be more forthcoming: boys do occasionally fancy girls, and vice versa. In Britain, by golly, even the villains are ever so chaste.

There is no outright colour prejudice either. The only black men I came across were in a publication called *Scorcher and Score*, and they were straight out of the Black and White Minstrel Show. Lord Rumsey, you see, was trying to raise money to save his mansion and his loyal staff, so he formed these good blacks into a football team and . . . but you get the drift. Lord Rumsey, you will not be surprised to hear, has a splendid moustache and wears a solar topee. The Empire lives—in *Scorcher and Score*.

The wars live, too. Fifty-three years have passed since the first world war, and twenty-six since the second, but bi-planes and evil Germans go on forever. *Lion and Thunder* tells us that:
German World War One ace Baron Maxilien von Klorr, known as Black Max, had trained giant killer-bats to tear British planes from the sky. He captured a recruit pilot, Johnny Crane, and turned him into a "human bat"! Then, using his "mind slave" to help him prepare a trap, Black Max captured his greatest enemy, Lieutenant Tim Wilson!

Another comic, called *Jet*, has an even more devastating tale:
To gain revenge for Germany's defeat in the Second World War, criminal scientist Doctor von Hoffman had invented a gas which enlarged all creatures and insects. He then embarked on a one-man invasion of Britain.

The same issue also has "the kids of Stalag 41" taking on a troop of stupid Gestapo: "I vant," says Herr Kolonel, "these spies captured at vunce! You heard . . . at vunce!"

This sort of thing could, of course, be portrayed as insidious anti-Common Market propaganda. But, of course, this isn't the intention. Germans and Japs make convenient villains; it saves having to draw them from swarthy ethnic minorities or, worse, from the ranks of the British aristocracy.

The impression one is, nevertheless, left with is that most of these strips are drawn by mysterious old men who miss the Empire, resent the need to be friendly with old enemies, want to keep blacks in their proper place, and firmly believe that nearly all problems are best settled by brute force.

Nor do they hold with women's lib. A weekly called *Princess Tina* has a heart-warming tale about Sue Day's Mum, who joined the Women's Liberation Movement and as a first sign of her freedom went for a week's holiday at a health farm. She simply *hated* it, and within a few days was back at the kitchen sink. "And that," Sue reports with a happy smile, "is the last we heard about women's liberation in our house!"

Snobbery seems to produce mixed feelings. On the one hand, we have *Scorcher and Score* giving a new role to royalty:
Bert Lacey, player-manager of Thornton Villa, had discovered that Rudolph Maximilian Rantzberg, the boy-king of Moravia, was a brilliant footballer and he was trying to make sure that Rudi returned to England to play for the Villa. . . .

On the other hand, *Bunty for Girls* does not hold with royal arrogance:
Sally Smith, a scholarship girl at Redford School, was told to help Princess

Rosetta of Centralia, a new girl. But Sally's job was to take all the punishment earned by Rosetta, who claimed that a princess could not be punished by commoners. . . .

The Princess and Sally are invited to visit the castle of a cockney peer who has made his money from supermarkets, calls them "ducks" and claims to be "ordinary Alf Higgins underneath." The Princess is appalled, and seizes an opportunity to chain him to one of the walls of his dungeon. Sally helps out, the Lord rewards her by taking her picture for a pre-packed food advertisement, and the headmistress arrives just in time to mete out suitable punishment to snooty Rosetta.

It seemed an appropriate moment to me to put aside the comics, and turn to teenage magazines like *Lover* and *Romance*. They are, happily, much less old-fashioned. There are no princesses romping through their pages, and no mad German scientists either. The world of Billy Bunter seems a million miles away. The editors clearly work on the assumption that their teenage readers are more interested in undies, deodorants and the eternal problem of how to keep a boy—or girl—from running off with someone else.

Sex dominates almost every page, but none of the magazines is ever likely to find itself prosecuted at the Old Bailey. "Some Day in Summer", a feature in this month's *Romance*, has a pretty young girl confessing: "I wanted to be sure of Noel—that was why I let him make love to me." But, of course, the episode had the traditional consequence: Janey found herself pregnant. Elsewhere, the magazine offers cunning advice on "How to get your holiday male," but this is tastefully balanced with sub-headings like "You can have the sofa, but be warned—there is a bolt on my door." Judge Argyle, I'm sure, would approve.

In the "heartcry section" of *Lover,* a troubled young lady wants to know if there is something wrong with her, and her boyfriend, because they have never discussed sex. "All the other girls," she explains, "say they're always being asked by their boyfriends to have sex." The reply is reassuring. "Some boys," we are told, "are satisfied to work out a mature and happy going-steady relationship before they think much about the sex bit. Others are different. But often it's a lot of talk. Your boyfriend's normal. You're normal too."

Fabulous, another weekly, defines what "being a girlfriend is":

Not wanting to go to the disco with your workmates anymore.

Spending your money on aftershave or a T-shirt for him instead of make-up and clothes for you.

Washing your hair on the night that he's at football.

Not wanting him to see you without your make-up.

Being nice to his family and putting up with his friends.

Getting used to the back seat of his scooter or his open top car.

Telling him he's wonderful—when he's happy and when he's down.

Nothing obscene there—unless, perhaps, you read more into that business about the back seat than you ought to. And not much in the way of corruption either.

This, of course, is precisely what magazines like *Oz* reject: the world of supergirl is no less distasteful to them than that of superkid. But it is obviously what young readers want; if not *Lover, Romance, Fabulous* and all the rest could hardly hold such formidable circulations.

For real protection, I am afraid, you will have to keep your children away not only from the Richard Nevilles, but from the daily stories of our adult world—violence in Northern Ireland, murder in My-Lai, persecution in South Africa, wife-swapping in Peyton Place. It means hiding the *Telegraph* under the sofa and banning the Nine o'clock News; it means explaining that long-haired young people have no monopoly on crassness.

On the other hand, you *could* just let them grow up in their own way.

"Very nice, Miss Hendrix, but I'm afraid we're over-stocked."

Look Out, Cézanne, the Market's Rising

ffolkes comes up with a new portfolio

"*. . . and this is his early period before they added Ingredient X*"

"*If you concentrate very hard it turns into a cheque for £50,000.*"

"*I hate to mention this, but there are two S's in Picasso.*"

"*Name's Van Gogh. Ahead of his time. Uncertain health. Buy now.*"

"*Gold leaf! More gold leaf!*"

How Miles Kington went to Cowes and Changed his Image

Punch Central Office is where they look after our image. Mostly it's just little things, like "Coren, get your hair cut" or "Put that secretary down," but once in a while it's a big job. I knew it was a big job last week when I was called to Central Office and the editor offered me some floor near his desk. I stood gratefully.

"We're going to have to re-think you, Kington," he said.

I could see he was angry about something. The little muscle was throbbing behind his left ear, which tells you when he is awake.

"I like myself as I am," I said huskily, flexing my sleeves and lighting a match. I looked hurriedly for my cigarettes.

Patiently, he ignored me.

"If you remember," he said, "we at Central Office started you bicycling just about the same time the Tories got Heath in his first boat. Now, he's Prime Minister, he's winning big races and his image is set fair. What's happened to your bicycling?"

"Had a good run this morning," I said. "Following wind till Knightsbridge, caught the flood tide at Hyde Park Corner, then a zippy port tack down Constitution Hill."

"I'll tell you what's happened. Your trousers have got oil-stains and you bore us all with your interminable biking yarns. Image-wise, nothing."

"I'm not sure I reckon these new-fangled Moultons," I said. "Oh, they're all right with a following wind and good visibility, but what use are those small wheels in squalls and deep puddles? Give me a heavy old Humber any day, with an easterly headwind coming down the Mall and the rain-clouds storming in across Nelson's shoulders."

"Tomorrow's your big chance, Kington. Heath can't go to Cowes for his race. But you can. We know a man who's got a boat. Tomorrow you become a sailor."

He turned away and wrote a quick article to signify the interview was over. Stunned, I wandered down the corridor and bumped into Coren.

"You keep your oily turn-ups to yourself," he snarled.

"I'm going racing at Cowes tomorrow," I said dully. "Any urgent messages can be left at the Island Sailing Club."

He goggled slightly and a new respect flickered across his face. By God, it's true, I thought; the image is improved already.

Minutes later I was speeding effortlessly by train, taxi and hovercraft to Cowes, where I spent a fascinating few hours locating the Island Club. The streets were thronged with wind-burnt men in blue clothes, strong and silent like grizzled waiters and none of them speaking English. Eventually I stopped an Australian sailor who explained to me with copious sign language that I was standing in, if not blocking, the entrance to the Club. It was there I met my two fellow crew members, Roy and Peter. They didn't speak English either.

"Halyard?" I said. "Starboard jib sheet? Fo'c'sle? L'ndl'bb'r? Qu'est-ce que c'est que tout ca?"

"Sorry, old boy," said Roy, "Quite forgot you didn't understand. We'll

59

tell you all about it before John turns up in the morning. He's the skipper, but he's at the Squadron Ball tonight."

After egg and sausage next morning he took me on a tour of the boat and explained in child's language how to hoist sails, get spinnaker booms up, control the jib, operate the topping-lift and meet Sir Max Aitken. By the end of it I felt that even if I still didn't know the ropes, I knew they weren't called ropes but sheets. Then John arrived, fresh from a few minutes sleep after the Ball, and reported on the great occasion. I didn't understand all the jargon, but it seemed that there had been a slight collision during the second waltz and a formal protest had been lodged.

We arrived shortly after ten in the main arena where the various races were due to start from, in the midst of a huge fleet of boats ranging from small dinghies to huge Admiral's Cup craft with trained teams of gymnasts arranged photogenically from fore to aft. Guns fired. Boats dashed off. Stop-watches were set. John had a beer. Roy stared through the binoculars.

"They've given us course 55," he reported.

"That's a long one—right down the Solent and into the sea," said John.

"I've arranged to meet my wife at 6.30," said Peter, apropos of nothing.

"You handle the winching handle on the jib winch, Miles," said Roy.

I said nothing.

"We're a bit over the line. We'll have to go back," said Roy.

"Prepare to go about," said John. I looked expectant. "Right, go about!"

The boat turned, sheets whistled, sails flapped.

"Wunchargdle!" yelled Roy. I looked interested. "WUNCHARGDLE!"

"Haven't you something a trifle more ostentatious?"

He pulled out the winching handle and thrust it at me. I tightened the winch and suddenly, from feeling small, I felt good.

"Correction," said Roy. "We weren't over the line at all."

Curses. Going about again. Swearing and depression, except for me who had got the winching handle in without prompting. Our starting gun fired and we headed for the distant starting line.

With all respect to Punch Central Office, as well as Mr. Heath, I think it's best to be the most junior on a boat. Let others argue the merits of various courses—catch a bit of wind here, avoid a bad tide there—and sit back in the cockpit, watching the sun come out slowly in complete defiance of the forecast and clutching the wunchargdle just in case.

"Put away that damned handle," said Roy.

Most of the boats in our class were ahead of us. We expected this, as ours was low in the classification and therefore had a good handicap. In fact there were only six boats reckoned to be slower, and there were six or more behind us. A good race. The boat level with us was called Braganza.

"Supposed to be faster, too," said Roy, consulting the library. "But they're not pointing as well as us." I looked a silent question. "They can't keep as close to the wind—they'll have to tack across before the next mark, then we'll be ahead. Got a job for you now, Miles."

I reached for the wunchargdle.

"You can make some lunch."

Down in the galley I made some s'rd'ne s'nd'ches. This is done by sliding the key in the loop and winching across the top of the tin, then unballasting the s'rd'nes on to packed bread while falling from one side of the galley to the other. Hours later I emerged.

"See that small black dot over there," said Roy.

"No," I said.

"That's Braganza."

I went below again to wash lettuce. When I reappeared, there was a boat just ahead. It was Braganza. John was issuing instructions for hoisting the spinnaker as soon as we rounded Bembridge Ledge. We went about, the jib came down but the spinnaker didn't go up. John cursed his crew for a pack of scurvy knaves. We smiled and sweated. The spinnaker went up but we had lost ground. Only four boats behind us now.

By four o'clock we were in front of Cowes again and heading past on the last leg. We had spent a leisurely afternoon thankfully packing the spinnaker away, watching Braganza pointing badly and getting wet as the forecast started to come true. It was then we realised that there were no boats behind us.

"They've all packed up and gone home," said Roy. "It's only us and Braganza now."

Braganza chose this moment to slide gracefully astern towards Cowes, waving.

"It's only us now," said Roy.

"Never mind," said John, "we'll have another go with the spinnaker on the homeward run."

There was silence.

"Said I'd meet my wife at 6.30," said Peter absently.

"Class I's having trouble with their spinnakers," said Roy vaguely.

"I sense that we have an anti-spinnaker faction on board," said John sternly. "You win."

"Belay there," I cried, leaping into Punch Central Office and spitting on the carpet. The editor looked up at my wind-swept features.

"Brush your hair," he muttered.

"Oh, it's you," he said. "Did you win?"

"It's a very complicated system of classification," I said. "But my wife looked at me with a new respect last night when I got back."

"Did you win?" he said sternly.

"Although we came last," I said, "I cannot describe to you the magic of being out in the spray, with the halyards slapping the mast and the creaking of the sheets. I have discovered a new world . . ."

"Last?" said Punch Central Office. "I have a new idea, Kington. Why not give bicycling another try?"

"*I've always wanted my own chat show.*"

****

I Could Have Talked All Night

MICHAEL PARKINSON discusses his life as a conversation piece

When it comes to pensionable occupations, hosting your own television talk programme is way behind lion-taming or being president of some banana republic. It is possibly the most dangerous job in the whole of the entertainment industry because it's the one job that everyone, the man in the boozer, "Disenchanted, Surbiton," your hairdresser and the critics (particularly the critics), believe they can do better. Nobody watches Frankie Howerd and says, "Piece of cake." No one watches Robin Day interviewing Mr. Heath and remarks "Like shelling peas," but everyone who watches a talk show believes that they have the edge on the man in the chair. One day they should be given the chance. The BBC should open its biggest studio to all those people who reckon they could make a name for themselves as a talk show host. They should be given a couple of people from Rent-a-Guest to interview and the result recorded. The BBC would then have a marvellous programme on its hands—so comically disastrous (of that I have no doubt) that a working title might well be "Don't Ring Us."

The basic trouble with a talk programme, the reason why people are misled into thinking it is so easy, is because it looks so easy. There is no production, no dancing girls, no tinsel sets. It's just a couple of chairs, a table and one or two people chatting on about this and that. I have often contemplated learning how to play the spoons and brushing up on a few conjuring tricks so that during those soggy bits in the talk when you can sense the audience getting restless I might stand up and give them a quick burst of "Marching Through Georgia" while pulling flags out of my guest's trousers. Failing that the real answer is to have an open-ended show, a set

of guests who have just arrived at the brandy stage and a genuine after dinner conversation during which various guests might get up to take a leak, burp, doze off, put their hand on their neighbour's knee and generally behave as normal people do in normal surroundings. It's a lovely thought, but like all the best ideas, it will never happen.

The fact is we're stuck with the old formula, the only difference being that the man in the hot seat is different and all we can do is hope to God that the public might spot the difference. Public apart, talk shows are fair game for satirists and the like. In my case, moving as I do between Fleet Street and Lime Grove, I sometimes meet the author of words that were designed to make me hurt and in a situation where we should circle one another, menacingly, like two gunslingers, we both look a bit embarrassed and pass the time of day. Critics and those they criticise should never meet. Inevitably they begin to like one another and the cutting edge is blunted.

Undoubtedly the most embarrassing situation of all is to literally walk into a plot being hatched against you. This happened to me only a few days ago in, of all places, the Punch office. I strolled in to attend Punch Table, popped into Miles Kington's office and felt a bit like a prefect who has discovered the Third Form Smoking Society. Papers were pulled out of the typewriters, drawers were slammed, cheeks I'd thought barren of blushes were tinged pink. After an uncomfortable few minutes, Kington told me that I had stumbled upon the composition of a send-up of my talk programme. "Who are my guests?" I asked. "Moses?" said Kington. "Too Jewish," I said and left him in his office

63

plucking at his double bass. Kington works diligently at being an eccentric and is one of the few men I know who is actually funnier in real life than in print.

What sustains the talk show host through everything is optimism, not to say blind hope. His life is based on it. On Monday he enters the office. "Who shall we have this week?" the producer asks. "Larry, Chuck Heston and Cardinal Heenan would be a marvellous mix," he says, the names tripping easily from the end of his tongue. "Sure," says the producer, "and if they fall down there's always Richard and Elizabeth, Jackie and Ari, Harold and Mary, you know—the loving couples programmes we talked about. Oh and Sophia's dying to do the show." The host nods and says, "It's a pity we've got things sewn up this week. Brigitte Bardot's in town, Katy Hepburn's filming in France and Charlie Chaplin's at home in Switzerland. It would make a great show." They head for lunch. Two days later, same office. Producer: "Larry's got laryngitis, Chuck's left town and Cardinal Heenan says some other time. Richard and Elizabeth are in Acapulco, Jackie and Ari are shopping in New York and Harold and Mary say not until their Cookbook is published. We're still in the market for Brigitte, Katy and Charlie though."

"Dinner's ready when you are."

Two days later, same office, now littered with beer cans, fag ends, crumpled paper. Producer: "I met a bloke in a bar last night who'd be marvellous for the show. He tap dances in wellington boots . . ." The point is no matter what the difference might be between Monday's dream and the weekend's reality, you can bet your shirt that next Monday they are still chasing Larry, Chuck and the Cardinal. The other problem of course is having booked your guests, how do you approach the interview and will they mix? The mixing is the most difficult and you know the moment they clap eyes on each other at run-through whether you are in for an easy ride or a trip through the petrified forest.

I once coupled a famous writer and a famous actor. Famous writer arrived late, walked on set and proceeded to denounce his wife, Ted Heath and the whole human race after being asked to do nothing more desperate than to give a sound level. "Don't have your bloody breakdowns in front of me," said famous actor. Famous writer: "I'm not going on with you, you're heartless." Exit famous writer and famous actor through opposite doors, leaving host feeling decidedly lonely and wondering how it would be if he interviewed himself for fifty minutes. But the great problem for the talk show host is how to digest all the advice and research he receives from a talented and dedicated team and at the same time be loose enough to play it by ear. The fascination of the exercise is the sheer unpredictability of the guests, particularly the thoroughbreds who can react to the prospect of talking about themselves to an audience of millions in extraordinary ways. The best example of this was when we interviewed Jacques Tati. Our researcher went to France and spent some time with Monsieur Tati. She reported back that he would talk about anything but would not, repeat not, perform any of his world famous mimes. He had pointed out, quite reasonably, that the mimes formed part of his music hall act and that once performed on television were dead for the theatre. Came the day and the interview. I thought I'd give it a try. We were talking about humour in sport, would Monsieur Tati demonstrate? He leapt to his feet and did his superb mime of a goalkeeper. Minutes later he demonstrated the difference between a French policeman and a bobby. We were delighted. After the show he came to me, his face full of despair, his shoulders heavy. "You didn't ask me to demonstrate enough. I should have done more," he said. Funny creatures, people who appear on talk shows. But not half so funny as the people who talk to them.

ANGLO-FRENCH PROJECTS

The Anglo-French TV panel game
In this brand new quiz, "Dix-neuf A La Douzaine," opposing teams of French and English personalities will keep a conversation going in the other's language, and try to understand what the other side is saying. Watch Frank Muir tackle the French r! Watch Spike Milligan mumble in a foreign language! Watch the Froggie team make unfair use of gestures! Watch Brigitte Bardot!

The Anglo-French newspaper
For the first time in one newspaper, French scandals about the Royal Family *and* the wit and wisdom of English leader writers. Also: French columns on great bitters for beer snobs, special supplements on the frog-growing industry, exclusive extracts from Desmond Morris's "Le Sexy Zoo" and letters from Dégoûté of Trouville.

The Anglo-French loaf

The Anglo-French musical
"English Can Can" tells the story of young Jean-Paul Hopkirk, who comes to Paris and London from the country and there makes his name as a top couture designer of raincoats. He conducts a long-distance romance on the telephone (song: "Allo? Dolly?") with a beautiful chorus girl doomed to die of a disease normally only contracted by camelias. He walks away under the umbrellas of Harwich, as Vera Lynn sings "Il y aura des oiseaux bleus au-dessus des sand-dunes de Calais."

The Anglo-French film
. . . In 1947, as France struggled to reconstitute its old pride and identity, a scholarly man walked into a left bank cafe reading a Camus novel, tripped over the recumbent form of Jacques Prevert and clutched for support at Simone de Beauvoir's skirts, which . . .

The Anglo-French policeman
Lovable, ferocious, helpful, corrupt, the Anglo-French policeman will go to any lengths to direct tourists to Piccadilly Circus, or, if time is short, beat them up there and then. There will be five basic ranks: Constable, Detective-Gendarme, Super-Maigret, Chief Bloodstainsman and Cop Supreme. The force will be known as the Cordon Bleu.

St. James's cockles
House paste
Soupe dans le tin anglaise
•
Snails and two veg
Supreme de rock salmon Cordon Bleu
Crapaud dans le trou
Roast horse et pudding Yorkshirais
•
Pudding de college
Dick avec des petites taches

The Anglo-French after-shave
"Shic" has that subtle blend compounded of a hint of garlic, a touch of wet cavalry twill, just a shade of anisette and a soupcon of smoky briar that make the girls say "Ouf!" Something incroyable happens when you use Shic. In the aerosol pack or the litre bottle.

The Anglo-French performer
A new artiste is already in training who will be able to appeal equally to French and English audiences. He will sing sweet English nothings in a French accent and vice versa, play superb flamenco guitar, juggle, dance and say "il y avait ce poulet qui traversait le chemin." He will probably be billed as Manitos de Frankie Distel, and always appear as a guest on his own show.

Monday

Was got up. Was given breakfast. Was told it was a nice morning.

Was just finishing my coffee when Philip arrived and said, "Shall we go and see what the score is?" This is a reference to our usual morning sport, viz. counting tourists outside railings. As it was sunny but cold, I forecast *nine*. He raised me five bob and forecast over *fifteen*. We went to look and there were only seven, so I was paid ten bob by P's equerry. One of them had a camera and was snapping everything in sight, viz. two sentries and enough tarmac to land a Concorde.

"Julius K. Hackenfeffer is alive and well, and keeping the Kodak company going," said Philip.

This a reference to the American tourist who is always outside our house, every day, come rain or shine. Sometimes he is bald, sometimes he is hairy, but he always answers to the name of Julius K. Hackenfeffer. He makes a lovely pet.

During the morning, I go for a walk in Buckingham Palace Gardens. Definitely the loveliest park in London. For one thing it is always empty, for another it is so convenient and near the house. Don't like St. James's Park or Green Park or Hyde Park, because you're not allowed to walk in them. Wonder what they're really like? Occasionally they let you ride down the Mall on a

horse, but always insist that you take a couple of Guards regiments with you. What a bore.

Worked late.

Tuesday

At 8 a.m., Julius K. Hackenfeffer had thirty Japanese friends with him. They were all photographing my house. Wouldn't it be cheaper to buy postcards of the view and save your film for somewhere more interesting? I know I would. Wish I had a camera.

Lunch at the Livery Hall of the Worshipful Seedsmen and Sundry Garden Toolers. Quite a nice little restaurant, though not in Good Food Guide. Admittedly, not great cooking, but for seven guineas you get three course meal plus five speeches which is quite reasonable. I found the service very good.

QUEEN'S LONDON

Was driven back via Embankment and Trafalgar Square. People complain about London traffic, but it never worries me. Whenever you think there's going to be a traffic jam, there's always a policeman ready to sort it out and I *never* get snarled up. Must get someone to phone a nice letter to *Evening Standard*.

In the evening went to the theatre. Not quite sure what the play was all about. Philip said it dealt with the problems of a group of actors who found themselves trapped in a long-running West End success. I never really enjoy the theatre, as we can never get good seats; we always end up in an awful box at the side, from which all you can see is the actors waiting to come on.

Worked late.

Wednesday

Did the weekly shopping list at breakfast. 300 avocado pears (having people in for dinner on Saturday), 2 prs kippers for Philip's Sunday breakfast, 1 new coach for formal visits, and *one camera*. Yes, I have decided to take the plunge.

Mother phoned during the morning from St. James's Palace. Can't think why she keeps that place on, with rates in central London being what they are. She always says that property is an investment and that her house would fetch a dozen times what she would have paid for it if she hadn't been given it. Yes, but would she ever find the right buyer? Just imagine: "Palatial residence near Piccadilly for sale. Many bedrooms, also original Van Dycks. Would suit heir to the throne or similar. £3,000,000 or nearest offer." I just couldn't bear seeing that dear little place given to Elizabeth Taylor for her 41st.

Had an outing this afternoon to see a new factory in Bletchley, where they make die-compressed plastic mouldings. Perhaps it was plastic-compressed die mouldings—I didn't listen as hard as I should have done. As outings go, it was quite fun; it certainly beats private showings of modern art all round. And it didn't take at all long by British Rail. Whatever you like to say about the railways, there's always a comfy seat waiting for you in an empty compartment, and there can't be many railways in the world that have carpeted platforms.

Worked late.

Thursday

Philip was down late for breakfast. When I asked him where he had been last night, he said gruffly: "I was dahn the East End, wasn't I?" Poor Philip—another boy's club, I suppose.

Went shopping for clothes before lunch in Harrods. Put on thick overcoat, dark glasses, tall hat, gloves and boots. Was intending to get new spring dress and flowery hat, but felt a bit stupid, so got new overcoat, fresh pair of dark glasses and boots.

This afternoon I went for a drive with my new camera! I took photos of gaping crowds in Trafalgar Square. Also gaping crowds in Piccadilly, gaping crowds in the Mall and gaping crowds in St. James's Street. Photography is not all it's cracked up to be.

Worked late.

Friday

Took my camera down to breakfast and photographed Philip at work on his egg, sausage and tomatoes. As soon as he heard the click of the lens shutter, a photogenic smile spread over his face and he said: "The art of photography has made terrific strides in the last two months. Its contribution to the world of communication can hardly be over-estimated. I therefore declare this darkroom well and truly open."

"Wake up, darling," I said. "It's only me. My Majesty."

"Oops," he said. "Thought I was in the P.S."

(This is our little joke. It means Public Sector. When we are being watched and one of us doesn't realise it, somebody says "P.S.".)

I showed him my photographs of tourists standing and gaping at me.

"What a life," I said. "They shuffle round all day in public, going from one Royal palace to another, having to look cheerful the whole time as if they're really enjoying it. I wouldn't do the job for a million pounds."

"I don't think it's really fair to criticise them," said Philip wisely. "After all, they can't answer back."

I was invited out to lunch today by the Royal Society of Water-Colourists and Aquatinters in Bloomsbury, which was nice of them, though I couldn't recall having met them. I tried to find Bloomsbury on the map we have framed in the sitting room, but in those days it seems to have been all fields beyond Charynge Crosse.

"Best way to Bloomsbury," said Philip, "is by a No. 3 Royal Car up Park Lane and Oxford Street, then change at Tottenham Court Road and the rest of the way by carpet."

Worked late.

Saturday

We are a bit worried about Julius K. Hackenfeffer, who has been absent for two days. Hope he's not ill.

The dinner went off as well as can be expected. Just five hundred of our friends and business contacts. Had a long and very interesting chat with a Japanese diplomat who hadn't been to London before. He liked it very much, as indeed did all of the five hundred whom I brought the subject up with. Especially he liked the Underground railway that everyone's always talking about.

Bit tired after the dinner, so didn't work late.

Sunday

Off to the country today! It will be nice to get to Sandringham again. I do love London but it's so noisy these days, what with the never-ending stamping of sentries' feet, the military bands, the clicking of shutters, and that sergeant shouting away.

As we drove out of the courtyard, I was relieved to see Julius K. Hackenfeffer back again and I gave him a smile and a wave. Unfortunately, he was looking into his camera and didn't see. Poor chap, I feel sorry for him on duty all over the weekend. Still, I expect he's used to the life by now.

You Called Me Baby Doll a Year Ago . . .

claims SALLY VINCENT

Before I embarked upon the inward journey by way of paper-back dream analyses, five-guineas-an-hour psychiatrists and R. D. Laing, I was free, as it were, to travel abroad in innocence. I imagined, in my simple way, that possession of passport, ticket and currency entitled me to the ambition of slopping around Mediterranean beaches inducing my body to go all toffee-coloured and my mind to broaden, gently as menopausal hips, to such information as Proust, Stendhal or Tolstoy have to offer.

Innocence, like ignorance, is nothing if not pretentious. Fortunately (or not as the case might be) it doesn't last; reality is constantly indecently exposing itself to those of us with impeccable motives and forcing out blameless eyes to gaze upon its monstrous face. I might *think* I'm a girl whose intentions are limited to sunbathing away an acne crop while taking in a novel, but what protection can my naive processes achieve against the fact that everyone else knows differently. She who sallies forth upon an inhabited beach is exhibiting herself for the sexual approval of males who believe, along with the mosquitoes, that her body is free. She is a willing rapee with no right even to select the identity of the rapist.

Sexual approach in these sunny circumstances is irrevocably entwined with sexual hostility, as I learned to the cost of twenty-seven and six when I was about seventeen. I was crouched harmlessly over the Dud Avocado on the banks of the Seine when one of those Algerian fellows with no forehead and gold teeth in the front elected to sit up against me as though there was an overcrowding problem and bad-breathed at me something approximating a deep and life-long alliance for the pair of us, commencing with a walk in the direction of his choice. Since my French was then fairly unequivocal I was able to enunciate clearly that I wished to be alone to read my book, thank-you and goodbye. But it wasn't until I had repeated my kindly phrases about nine times that I realised he had painstakingly burned a huge hole in my skirt with his Gauloise.

In the years following this initiation I learned to defend myself with less linguistics. I can say "I do not speak" in eight languages and I'm working on a ninth. Unfortunately this method is not always successfully repelling. I remember, particularly, an ugly scene on the beach at Malaga, when I was beaten about the head and shoulders with a superman comic by a young Spaniard in a frenzy of frustration because to his fuddled little brain "no ablar Espagnol" meant precisely the reverse. If you know three words, he reasoned beneath his black hair and religious medallions, you know them all. Which, strange as it might seem, is a sentiment not uncommon among beach boys. Many of them go to the strain of equipping themselves with a formidable list of three-worders, so that when "are—you—Engleesh?" hits the spot they reckon themselves half way to your hotel bedroom. Hell hath no fury like a beach boy when you tell him you're waiting for a friend and some have extended their vocabulary to include such exit lines as "you are fat," "you are thin," "you are mean" and "you are old."

I must, however, confess that even in the midst of such habitual and squalid encounters, I still believe romance is to be found on foreign soil.

Indeed, once upon a time and very far away in a place I shall call, for the sake of respectable anonymity, Greece, I fell madly in love with a correctly introduced and splendidly handsome young man. I knew from the way he clicked his heels together and made a little bow from the

"*I haven't yet finalised the details but you're going to be something very big down here somewhere.*"

neck that he was a serious person. Our relationship, to put it mildly, blossomed, wonderfully assisted as it was by the fact that his English was none too brilliant. We were, therefore, unable to indulge ourselves in the sort of disillusioning communication occasioned by the sophistry of a mutual tongue. Romance, as everyone knows, thrives on little mysteries like not knowing the first thing about each other. Three weeks passed in a kind of light-headed paradise, stabilised only by my absolute certainty that I had met Mr. Right and there remained only a few details such as immigration, marriage and repatriation between me and happy-ever-after. I was, of course, peacefully discouraged from checking the efficacy of my dreams against the broken English of any kind of a response.

One day, in the full flood of my passion, I found myself alone in his apartment while he was out buying me yet another token of his esteem. Time was feather-light in my hands as I revelled in the presence of the possessions of the loved-one, engrossed in that frenetic awareness of things where an object, such as a collar stiffener, takes on a beautiful significance that has previously, in one's other blindly loveless state, been elusive. My absorption in the trinkets of his daily life gradually developed, not to put too fine a point on it, into a desire to snoop. Drawers and cupboards became open drawers and cupboards and busy little fingers were rapidly rifling their contents.

The prize find was a parcel of letters which I shamelessly made available to myself, sorting the English from the foreign and gobbling up their messages in hysterical haste lest the door open and my fervent dedication mistaken for an obscene disrespect for privacy.

They were, as luck would have it, all love-letters. Love-letters, indeed, of a singular quality, somewhat banal in style and high-pitched in tone. "My pillow is wet with tears because you are no longer in my arms," was the kind of thing. And "sweet pussycat I long for a glimpse of your beauty." It was compulsive, even hot, stuff but there was something intangibly *odd* about them all that I could not explain to myself as mere lack of literacy. It was not until I had snaffled up the tenth—"will I ever forget the joy of your embrace"—that a signature caught my eye. "Robert," it said. Quite distinctly. I checked through the pack. "John," they had written, "Martin," "Claude," "Richard." There was no question about it, I was the only woman in his life. Which might have been some comfort to me on the flight home. No, one will never again travel innocently. But hopefully is always another matter.

. . . Who, Me?

bleats STANLEY REYNOLDS

No holiday is complete without romance. Tanned hands I held across a plate of squid overlooking the harbour at Corfu! The billets doux delivered by uniformed flunkey to the lady in red at the baccarat table that wicked August in Monte. The one perfect rose your chauffeur brought each morning to the lonely Baroness with the eyes just made for tears at that white villa by the green vineyard. The secretary from Skegness who got sick on your shoes after too much ouzo.

But to begin at the beginning. We were having one of those English summers when even the rain has a bite in it and I had just sent all my summer wear to the cleaners and my continental slip-ons to the cobbler when the cable came from Harvey Undergrowth ordering me to jet out to Roma and meet him at Cinecitta to talk over the film treatment we had just penned for Louis M. Osterlitz Junior. The only thing left in my wardrobe was an iron clad Harris Tweed in heather mixture and a pair of Northampton hobnailed lace-up brown boots. Little did I know that a period of great romance was waiting for me as I skied into Rome and stood sweltering under that Dago sun in my Harris Tweeds. To

*"Where do all these pedestrians **come** from? I'm sure at least half of them are unnecessary."*

give you some idea of the picture I cut, Lena Spinoza, the fabled D cup of all those spaghetti westerns of the early 'Sixties, was hanging on Osterlitz's arm and she looks at me and sneers at Osterlitz, "Who's this-a script write you buy-a for me, caro, Rudyardo Kipoling?" They took one look at Harvey's co-author and bugged off to the sun, sand, and sea of the Italian Riviera.

"Listen," Harvey says to me, "a joke's a joke, kiddo, but coming on like Richard Hannay in The Thirty Nine Steps is just too much."

"What's wrong, kiddo?" I asked trying to make up in the vernacular what I lacked in visual presentation.

"This is the hip, cool, swinging film world," he says. "La Dolce whatcha call it. You fall out in that suit and them brogues and Easy Rider you ain't."

Harvey whipped me around to a Roman haberdashery and got me kitted out in candy floss pink velvet pants, a see-through black lace shirt, and a pair of satin sneakers and we motored south in pursuit of Osterlitz.

"That's terribly civil of you, miss," I said, "my name is Hannay, Dick Hannay. Dashed crowded here, what? Think a chap could get such a thing as a cup of tea. Make a fella feel more like a white man."

"Oh, gosh, yes," the other girl says, "I've been here two months and now I know what it is I've missed all the time—a nice cup of tea."

"I daresay you do, Miss," I said, "but what I'd like to hear is the crack of willow. Any news of the Test?"

"Oh, oh," the one called Samantha cried like I'd just offered her my villa at Cannes, "the Test!! Golly, how super" and she cuddled up to me feeling the hell out of my tweed sleeve.

All the time, of course, Zeppo and Chico are eyeing me up wondering what's what. They can see right away I'm the same mug in the erstwhile black lace and pink trews but their English isn't good enough to catch what's going on. I slipped the dagoes a conspiratorial wink. Zeppo started yawning again. I think he was glad about getting the night work off his hands. But Chico looked away and pretended to spit.

"I go Londra," Chico said loudly trying to save the day, "I work—a trattoria Inglesa. I serve—a fish, I serve—a cheep."

Samantha and Cynthia ignored him, it is amazing how steely hearted they can be when something a little more super rolls in. By the end of the week I had collected eight English roses who were so home sick for England they took my summer-of-1914 persona for the real thing. Of course it cost me a few dozen bunches of flowers but that was the sort of Robert Donat-Walter Pidgeon thing I had to do and it was hot work leaping up to pull out and push in chairs in the heather mixture tweeds. Still, there is a lot to say for old style romance particularly when you reach that marvellous stage when you no longer call her Miss Smith or Miss Huntington-Farquar

70

and must, due to circumstances beyond control of your stiff upper lip, whisper Samantha or Cynthia in her ear. And it was worth it. Worth all that endless talk about English hedgerows, cabbage whites, tea, and the rain in Manchester just to see the look of wondering disbelief on the Eyeties when Mister Nothing came down to the beach in braces flanked by dollies galore for a little seaside cricket with an old tennis ball and a slab of driftwood.

Had I stayed any longer I think I might have done some good for the Scottish weaving industry but as it was I had just enough time to hot foot it back to Rome and the Cinecitta studios to tell Osterlitz and Undergrowth to stuff their film. Osterlitz was sitting sweltering in a big tweed suit with Lena beside him in twin set and pearls. "Don't get hasty, kiddo old chap," he said, "I like your style, Lena likes your style. Dash it all, baby, don't be hasty." But with all the weight I had lost sweating in that suit I was dying to get back to the Serpentine in my skin tight candy floss pinks and bring a whiff of the Med to Gabriella, Gina, Yole, Bianca, and the rest of the au pairs.

So all day long Harvey was chasing after Osterlitz and all day I am lounging on the beach trying to lure the girls with my thirty-eight-inch waist and moon pale torso but for some silly reason they seem to prefer the dark skinned local products with nineteen-inch waistlines and sculptured profiles. At night I sit in a cafe and sip seventeen or eighteen large whiskies while romance and the beach bums arm in arm with all the available talent pass me by.

But three days out I learn two things. First, I am getting the shakes drinking all that whisky and second, all these girls were English. All the foreign bimboes it seems were in London working as au pairs and sunning themselves in the mist by the Serpentine when they get a day off from being pinched by the Monsieur.

Anyway one night two English girls who I had been eyeing all the time come into the crowded cafe with a brace of beach bums and sit at my table. I had been getting out at first light trying to attract a tan that might possibly compete but looking at Zeppo and Chico Marx sitting there at my table I see I would have had to start around about back in the summer of '42 to catch up with the home grown items. I had offered to wash Osterlitz's Maserati one day hoping to pass myself off as a big man in the talkies but evidently every phoney on the Riviera has tried that stunt. I had been thinking too about getting a camera and going around as a photographer

from *Weekend Tidbits* but a Kodak Box Brownie is apparently not fooling them this year either.

I had just about made up my mind to join Harvey in talking Osterlitz around on the film deal when suddenly Franco or Zeppo yawns and stretches himself and one big tanned arm knocked my drink right into my lap soaking the pink skintights right through.

There was nothing for it but to limp back to the hotel and change into the heather mixture tweeds. Back in the room I got into the suit and suddenly I caught a reflection of myself in the mirror. It was like a stranger looking back at me but then I looked again and I saw this stranger was familiar. It was Mr. Chips, it was Walter Pidgeon as Mr. Miniver, it was Richard Hannay, young John Bull, it was England, the England of drizzling rain, country lanes, nice hot cups of tea, and village cricket looking right out at me.

Now there are one or two times in a man's life when he can't seem to do anything wrong and this was both of those times for me. Soon as I fell in back at the table with Zeppo, Chico, and the English dollies I could see something was new. What it was was me. I could see me shining right there in all four of those English blue eyes. "This seat is free," one of the girls says, right away, "there was some sort of middle-aged swinger here but he left."

"Hey kid! How'd you like to be a star in the movies?"

British Isles plus one
THE BRITISH ISLES increased by one yesterday, when a new island appeared off the Isle of Wight, one mile north-west of the Needles. Coastguards explained there had been a shingle bank there for some years—"but it must have built up, and is now three or four feet out of the water," he said.

AN ISLAND IS BORN

and with it, a unique opportunity to study the British in action

This is the only part of Britain that has no history, no heritage. It gives social scientists a chance to study, in laboratory conditions, the Briton's reaction to his own country. And to verify the following twenty propositions

1. The nearest mainland property owner will hire a lawyer to prove it is his.

2. A humorous letter will be written to The Times about the British Empire having reversed its deflationary trend and started to expand again.

3. A serious letter will be written to The Times pointing out that as it has become a staging post for the Lesser Spotted Guillemot, it should be designated a bird sanctuary.

4. The island will be bought by a whisky or corn flake firm and given away as a prize. Say in not more than fifteen words why you would like to own your own landmass, and range Greenland, Madagascar and Fiji in order of importance.

5. It will be developed residentially by a speculator. "Unique estate near Isle of Wight, some properties still remaining, with immediate access to sea and beautiful sands." There will be more to "some properties still remaining" than meets the eye.

6. The boating fraternity will label it a hazard to shipping and prevail upon the Fleet Air Arm to bombard it. In an action lasting less than three hours it will be blasted into non-existence. There will be few casualties.

7. Pat Arrowsmith will retire there for a nuclear scare.

8. Someone will conceive the idea of holding a pop festival there. It will not get beyond the committee stage.

9. An Isle of Wight boatman will organise trips round the island.

10. Next Christmas, every newspaper's festive quiz will ask: "Which island came into the news for the first time this year?"

11. The first structure to be erected on the new island will be a signpost reading: "WARNING TO BATHERS: OIL ON BEACH."

12. Private Eye will print exclusive information on the scandalous uses to which the new island will be put.

13. Private Eye will apologise for having printed false information concerning the new island and Reginald Maudling, Peter Walker, W. H. Smith's, The Spectator and Neasden.

14. There will be a move to have it designated "an area of outstanding natural beauty" to prevent it being demolished by unscrupulous building materials contractors.

15. Its photograph will appear prominently in the Guardian, The Sun will organise a competition to find a name for it, and Bernard Levin will calculate that the population of the Isle of Wight could stand on it comfortably.

16. Nine authors will simultaneously start work on nine books to demonstrate that it is the lost world of Atlantis and/or King Arthur's Camelot.

17. A luxury hotel will not be built there and Alan Whicker will not devote a programme to it.

18. After several years of life, the island will have acquired: ten drums of poisonous chemicals, one rubber tyre, four Schweppes bottles, a pair of sunglasses, a piece of flotsam inscribed "E H 1972" and a dead seagull.

19. Everyone will forget about it.

20. It will vanish one day beneath the waves.

*"What does he mean—a pint of **ordinary** bitter?"*

HIGH NOON REVISITED

By CARL FOREMAN

From: CARL FOREMAN
To: S.K., S.L., S.S., S.J., S.P., S.W.J., S.U., S.Z.S., S.F. and S.X.W.
Subject: "HIGH NOON" REMAKE

Classic, shmassic. As both Carl Laemmle, Sr., and Louis B. Mayer said on various occasions, we have to keep up with the times. In other words, change our act or go back to the woods. I take it that none of us is really hankering for the Thoreau bit, no matter what is said in the men's room after conferences, so perhaps we'd all better get on the ball and see if it flies up to the penthouse. It's exactly twenty years since we first released *High Noon*, which means that by any standards it's remake time down at the back lot, what's left of it, so, gentlemen, I suggest we get on our horses and shove off.

But the key to the whole thing lies in the first two words of the paragraph above. What I mean is, if I'm willing to say let's not treat the original with exaggerated respect, the rest of you ought to be able to think of the picture in contemporary terms, too, bearing in mind what's being made today, what's selling today, and what the bulk of our audiences are: young, sophisticated, aware people who not only know the truth about the world today but want to see it on the screen as well. They want to *relate* to it. That means that the picture has to be *sincere*. And it means that we have to show the west as it really was, and not the way I and all the others glorified it twenty years ago. But the marvellous thing is that this is a story that can easily be brought up to date, as I now propose to demonstrate.

However, first I would suggest that we start being sincere with the casting. My own feeling is that up to six months ago Sidney Poitier or

"Try not to get involved, Henry."

73

Harry Belafonte or that fellow in *Shaft* would have been right on for the Marshal, but we may have reached saturation on the black bit, and I suspect that there is some feeling that we ourselves have not been exactly sincere in this regard. So I suggest we more or less cool black is beautiful on this role, and we might well be boxing clever if the Marshal is Puerto Rican or, how about this, a Jordanian Arab? I like Twiggy for the Grace Kelly part, and the Katy Jurado role could be played by a Mexican girl again or Shirley Bassey or Diana Ross and any one of the Supremes. This would give us a pretty good racial spread without making it look too obvious, and we would also have going for us the fact that the town's establishment and power structure would all be Wasps. So, so far so good, agreed?

So, the story begins as before with these three yobs riding into town, only this time they're three butch poofs. On their way to the railroad they pass the Marshal's office where, in the original, the Marshal and the little Quaker broad are getting married. We'll have to change the marriage ceremony to something more contemporary, perhaps a handshake deal, or something. It's a detail. The three skinheads continue on past the brothel, where the Marshal's Deputy and the Madame, Helen Ramirez, are just rolling out of the hay. Note: we go very light on this, so we can save our big guns for later. Just a little flash, and all in good taste.

Anyway, now comes the part where the Marshal learns who is coming in on the noon train, and he starts looking for help. Naturally, the little Quaker broad thinks he has flipped and walks out on him.

First, the Marshal goes to his friend the newspaper publisher. This representative of capitalist decadence is engaging in some bondage and other sado-masochist sex-play with his brow-beaten wife, her French maid and the Tweeny, and won't even come to the door. Next he goes to the miner's club-house where some of the younger and more progressive members are courageously breaking taboos and engaging in some bondage

"Don't look now, old man, but I think we're being followed."

"It's not poverty I mind. It's the ceaseless hammering."

and other sado-masochist sex-play, and they have no time for him. He goes to see his old pal, the one who had the Marshal's job before him. He finds him on a couch smoking an opium pipe, while the young wet-back cat he is keeping sits in a corner rolling sticks of pot. A great scene, in which the former pig tells our hero the real truth about law and order. I think a great casting coup for this role would be John Wayne, especially now that he is playing character parts. I realise Duke thinks that any picture without a cattle-drive is un-American, but considering how much he liked *High Noon* when it first came out, I think he could be talked into this one.

Anyway, while all this is going on, the little Quaker broad starts down to the station and gets herself gang-raped on the way by a bunch of Apache urban guerrillas. Here we can combine the best elements of the rape sequences in *Straw Dogs* and *A Clockwork Orange,* and I remind you that we have a great music library and we could use one of our own numbers, say *Born Free,* while the little girl is getting the old in-and-out from the redskins. When they tire of her, they toss her onto the front steps of the brothel, where—no, wait for it.

Meanwhile, our hero goes to the church, and arrives right in the middle of a Black Mass. The children are all sent out to play, and we follow them for a marvellously nauseating sequence in which they hang, draw and quarter live chickens in a nearby backyard. And here, in all modesty, I put to you a great idea: what we do here is we intercut frozen frames of an execution in mediaeval England in which *human beings* are having the same things done to them. This will show that we really abhor violence, and that our picture is really anti-violence, and I'm sure that the value of this sequence, in terms of good, deep, box-office reviews by the serious critics is obvious to all of you.

But, back to the church where, naturally, the people are a little sore at being interrupted just as things were getting interesting, and they give our friend the Marshal short shrift. Indeed, in their annoyance, they are about to give him the full treatment with the ceremonial dildo, but he manages to break away and dive through a stained-glass window depicting the Crucifixion (not a bad touch, right?), and make his way, as before, to a stable. This was where we originally had the great fight scene with his Deputy, but we can improve on it. We can indicate that these two were once lovers, and the Deputy is simply furious about being dumped for the little Quaker dish. So he knocks out the Marshal, ties him up, and strips him and

"And that's not all about the punishment block—they've installed piped music!"

whips him good. And, at the very same time, back at the brothel, the little Quaker crumpet is brought into the Madame's suite. Helen has her washed off and up, and she likes what she sees. In no time at all, these two are in each other's arms, not to mention legs. We've been restrained until now, but the picture is approaching its climax (ha-ha) and it's time we gave the customers what they want when they say movies are better than ever.

Back at the stable, fantastic. The horses go mad with the scent of blood, break loose and trample the Deputy to a bloody dead splotch, right before our eyes, and then stampede. The Marshal comes to, and frees himself. He staggers to the local burial parlour, where the Undertaker is embalming the naked corpse of a recently deceased saloon dancing-girl, and the stiff-stuffer grudgingly lets our hero get cleaned up.

From here on the story remains much the same. The train arrives at high noon, and off comes the heavy: a circus strong-lady about seven feet tall, with a full beard. If we can't find a real one in the US, maybe we can borrow some Russian lady hammer-thrower, or, as a last resort, maybe we could ask Tony Quinn to play it in drag, just for laughs. Back at the brothel, the two girls zip themselves up, and hurry to help the Marshal. Now comes the big shoot out, but this we have to modernise and cuten up. I mean, steel traps like in *Straw Dogs* maybe setting the bad guys on fire with molotov cocktails like in *Diamonds Are Forever*, stuff like that. I mean, it's a challenge, but we ought to be able to improve on what we borrow, and give our audience a real rousing ending.

So all four bad guys are dead. Now, in the original the Marshal and his wife up and left town. In the contemporary version, I put it to you that it would be more satisfying, as well as more sincere, if the Marshal, the Quaker broad and the Madame all go and live together in the brothel. They have all been through the crucible together, they have been tried and not found wanting, and they have the right to some decent happiness together. We do some beautiful slow motion shots as they play with themselves in the bathroom, just like children, simple and uncomplicated, and we end on a freeze frame of the three of them in bed.

Gentlemen, I put it to you, this could be our big picture of the year. Furthermore, the way things are, we're almost sure to get a U certificate, or, at worst, an A, and I think we should sell it as a family picture.

"It wouldn't be so bad if he bought something now and then!"

FORWARD!

SUN-TIMES-EXPRESS

11 August 1981

WHAT ABOUT NEW ZEALAND? CRY FROM WILLI BRANDT

Unprecedented German Statement As Europroduction Drops

ON continentwide Eurotelevision last night, amid uproar following the announcement of a further drop in production to less than a one per cent growth over last year's figures, Herr Willi Brandt claimed that he had never said that he was in favour of Germany's being in the Common Market. "I said I would stay in only if the terms were right," he told viewers, and affirmed that most of his supporters, if they searched their memories, would concur that

Herr Brandt had always worried about the economic prospects for New Zealand.

Since Britain's entry into the EEC, Europe's economic growth rate has steadily declined, while inflation has rocketed, and observers are generally agreed that this situation is what lies behind Herr Brandt's recent attempts to get talks started on German entry to the British Commonwealth. Last night, he went on: "There is a tremendous potential for growth in a solid economic bloc made up of Australia, New Zealand, Canada, Africa and India. Europe cannot exist alone in the twentieth century. Germany has age-old wartime ties with the Commonwealth, and I shall do my utmost to see that those ties are consolidated. Only in this way can we effectively combat the economic threat of America and Japan and the Soviet bloc." Asked whether, if Germany's Commonwealth entry was succesful, he would like to see Great Britain get out of Europe and back into the Commonwealth, Herr Brandt fell off his chair and was (continued page 3)

His Holiness the Pope, during his guest appearance last night on The Golden Shot, *when he appealed for funds to repair the Vatican roof. Speaking of the wave of religious apathy which has swept Europe so suddenly over the past few years, His Holiness carefully refrained from laying blame, but pointed out that when Sammy Davis Jr. was being paid £20,000 a night for appearing at St. Peter's Workingmen's Club, Rome, then mankind had surely somehow taken a wrong turning.*

ORIENT EXPRESS FORTNIGHT LATE

Starving Commuters Run Amok

Trieste, Monday

COMMUTING Europe was gripped by rail chaos for the fourteenth successive day yesterday when the 9.15 train from Haywards Heath to Istanbul still failed to arrive.

Belgian workers who had travelled from Ghent to Trieste a fortnight ago to make the connection with the 9.15 (scheduled to take them to shipyard work in Brindisi) clashed last night in Trieste station buffet with Neapolitan supporters of F. C. Salerno who have been waiting for ten days to pick up the *returning* Orient Express (i.e. the 7.30 from Istanbul to Haywards Heath) to take them to Nantes for the semi-final of the European Fairs Cup, which in fact took place last Tuesday. The clash is believed to have been over the disputed ownership of the last bath bun in Trieste, on which the deranged travellers hoped to

subsist for a few hours more

As the Trieste waiting-room burned, maddened Hanoverian accountants stranded in Dubrovnik by the delay which has upset timetables all over Europe turned on a Yugoslav delegation who have been waiting for a week to pick up the Rome Express due to carry them to Zeebrugge for the European Fishing Rights Conference which ended yesterday; while, in Geneva, the Indian Test Team having waited for two weeks for the connection necessary to take them to their fixture against Sussex at Hove, applied this morning for Swiss citizenship.

A spokesman for Southern Region, asked today to comment on the Haywards Heath hold-up said: "It's probably frozen points at Didcot, or it could be rail warp somewhere due to unexpected warm weather. We're looking into it."

the Common Market. But what about the effect on *Europe?*

The latest stretch of the A65 Autobahn designed to link Hamburg to Munich, completed yesterday, which fell down this morning, thirty miles outside Madrid. A spokesman for the British firm handling the contract was optimistic: "It's extremely fortunate the autobahn was built in the wrong place. If it collapses near Madrid, it affects no-one, whereas had it collapsed somewhere between Hamburg and Munich, it could have proved most embarrassing." Asked for reasons why the structure itself was faulty, he went on: "Over-eagerness on our part, beyond a doubt. We were hurrying to complete the contract before the penal clauses, which began to take effect three years ago, became too heavy. Also, we ran short of prime materials while we were building the unexpected Lisbon by-pass, and three of our suppliers went bankrupt during the construction of the Pyrenean tunnel. But if the weather holds, we have every hope of being in Oslo before Christmas."

Volkswagen to Close
Receiver Called In

VOLKSWAGEN, once the most successful motor-car company in the world, announced last night that it is to cease production. An official receiver has been appointed to wind up the company's affairs.

This disaster, and the attendant loss of more than 100,000 jobs, is directly due to the eighteen-month stoppage at the Hailwood plant of Jas. Fibley & Co., the English firm which manufactures the Volkswagen petrol-filler-cap, or, rather, did until the dispute which brought production to a halt a year-and-a-half ago. The dispute arose after the firm's decision to pack the filler-caps in polystyrene boxes rather than in the traditional wooden crates previously used, which meant the redund-

ancy of the firm's carpenter, Mr. Esmond Fince, whose union immediately called the stoppage.

The 470,000 VW cars which have been stockpiled outside Frankfurt since the beginning of the strike will probably be sold for scrap.

OBERAMMERGAU RIOT
Nude Apostles Flee Audience Wrath

THE Oberammergau Passion Play came to an abrupt halt today when members of the audience, incensed at the notorious full frontal sequence of the woman taken in adultery, stormed the stage and began pelting the naked cast mercilessly. Attempting to calm the situation, Ken Russell, the director, rushed onstage and cried: "Let him who is without sin cast the first stone." He was knocked flat by a brick. (*Reuter*)

AUSTRIAN'S MASSIVE BINGO WIN

Frau Eva Igelsdreck, 43, wife of a former Bregenz platelayer, last night won a record £31,466 at the Wienerbingohallundeinarmbanditspalast, formerly the Vienna State Opera House.

BAUDOUIN CROWNED IN EXTRA TIME THRILLER !

THE first season of the Eurovision Monarchy Contest, set up last year to establish royal precedence in Europe on an annual basis, was won last night after extra time in a thrilling contest between King Baudouin of Belgium and Queen Juliana of the Netherlands, with King Baudouin declared the winner, 3-2. The final table for the contest, which takes the form of darts games in the back room of the Rat and Cockle, Bolsover, reads as follows:

	P	W	D	L	Pts
Baudouin	6	4	1	1	9
Juliana	6	3	1	2	7
Frederik	6	3	0	3	6
Elizabeth II	6	2	1	3	5
Gustav VI	6	1	0	5	2
Olav V	6	0	1	5	1

Note An application by Grand Duke Jean of Luxembourg to enter next year's contest was once again turned down by the International Royal Darts Committee.

ALL YOU NEED TO K

GERMANY

The People
Germans are split into two broad categories: those with tall spikes on their hats, and those with briefcases. Up until 1945, the country's history was made by those with spikes. After 1945, it was made by those with briefcases. In common with the rest of Europe, its history is therefore now known as economics. Ethnically, the Germans are Teutonic, but prefer not to talk about it any more. This ethnos was originally triform, being made up of Vandals, Gepidae, and Goths, all of whom emigrated south from Sweden in about 500 BC; why they emigrated is not exactly clear, but many scholars believe it was because they saw the way Sweden was going, i.e. neutral. Physically, Germans are tall and blond, though not as tall and blond as they sometimes think, especially when they are short, dark Austrians with a sense of destiny. When they sing, the Germans link arms and rock sideways; it is best described as horizontal marching.

The Land
The country, or *Lebensraum*, is extremely beautiful and situated in the very centre of Europe, thus lending itself to expansion in any direction, a temptation first succumbed to in the fifth century AD (the *Volkerwanderung*) when Germany embraced most of Spain, and regularly indulged in since. It is interesting to note that this summer there will be three million Germans in Spain, thus outnumbering the first excursion by almost a hundred to one.

The History
For almost two thousand years, Germany was split into separate states that fought one another. In the nineteenth century, they combined and began fighting everyone else. They are currently split up again and once more fighting one another. If they combine, the result is anybody's guess. Having lost the last war, they are currently enjoying a *Wirtschaftswunder*, which can be briefly translated as "The best way to own a Mercedes is to build one." That is about all there is to German history, since no one has ever known what was going on, and if this is the case, then the Truth cannot be said to exist. Germany has, as you can see, provided many of the world's greatest philosophers.

BELGIUM

The People
Belgium is the most densely populated country in Europe, and is at the same time fiercely divided on the subjects of language and religion. This means that it is impossible to move anywhere in the country, which is packed with mobs standing chin to chin and screaming incomprehensible things at one another in the certain knowledge that God is on their side, whoever He is. That there has not been more bloodshed is entirely due to the fact that there isn't room to swing a fist. Consequently, what the Belgian authorities most fear is contraception: if it ever catches on, and the population thins to the point where rifles may be comfortably unslung from shoulders, the entire nation might disappear overnight.

The Land
The land is entirely invisible, except in the small hours of the morning, being for the rest of the time completely underfoot. It is therefore no surprise to learn that Belgium's largest industries are coal and mineral mining, as underground is the only place where there is room to work. Plans have been suggested for reclaiming land from the sea, on the Dutch pattern, but were always shelved as soon as it was realised that there was neither room for the water that would have to be removed from the sea, nor, alternatively, any spare land to spread to extend the coastline outwards.

The History
Belgium has always suffered horribly at the hands of occupying forces, which, given the overcrowding, is only to be expected. The bayoneting of babies by Prussians, for example, was never intentional; it was simply that it was impossible to walk about with fixed bayonets in such confined spaces without finding something stuck on the end of them. For the same reason, the sprout was developed by Brussels agronomists, this being the largest cabbage a housewife could possibly carry through the teeming streets.

FRANCE

The People
The French are our closest neighbours and we are therefore bound to them b bonds of jealousy, suspicion, competi tion, and envy. They haven't brough the shears back, either. They are short blue-vested people who carry their ow onions when cycling abroad, and have a yard which is 3.37 inches longer tha other people's. Their vanity does no stop there: they believe themselves t be great lovers, an easy trap to fall int when you're permanently drunk, an the natural heirs to Europe. It has bee explained to them that there is a differ ence between natural heirs and legiti mate heirs to Europe, but they cannot appreciate subtle distinctions, probably because French has the smallest vocabulary o any language in Europe.

The Land
France is the largest country in Europe a great boon for drunks, who need room to fall, and consists of an enormous number of bars linked by an intricate system of serpentine cobbles. Exactly why France is so cobbled has never been fully explained, though most authorities favour the view that the French like to be constantly reminded of the feel of grapes underfoot. The houses are all shuttered to exclude light, as a pre caution against hangovers, and filled with large lumpy beds in which the French spend 83.7 per cent of their time recovering from sex or booze or both The lumpiness is due, of course, to the presence of undeclared income under the mattresses.

The History
French history, or "gloire" starts with Charlemagne, and ends with Charlemagne. Anything subsequent was in the hands of bizarre paranoiacs who thought they were God (Louis XIV) or thought they were Charlemagne (Napoleon) or thought they were God and Louis XIV and Charlemagne and Napoleon (de Gaulle). Like most other European nations, the French have fought everyone, but unlike the rest have always claimed that both victories and defeats came after opposition to overwhelming odds. This is probably because they always saw two of everything.

To help you, we have prepared this handy cut-out-and-keep wallchart.

OW ABOUT EUROPE

LUXEMBOURG

People

re are nine people in Luxembourg,
they are kept pretty busy making
ps. It is not the smallest country
urope: there are only eight people
Monaco, five in Andorra, and Herr
. Klausner in Liechtenstein, so as
fourth non-smallest country in
ope, it enjoys a rather unique posi-
. The people are of middle height,
the small, deft fingers of master-
rators, and all look rather alike,
ept for their Uncle Maurice who
an ear on the Somme. They are a
er arrogant people (they refer to
ld War I as the Battle of Maurice's
) but not unartistic: *My Day At The*
by the country's infant prodigy,
into nine copies and won the Prix
urice for 1969.

Land

a clear day, from the terrace of the
on de Philatelie, you can't see
embourg at all. This is because a
is in the way. Beyond the tree lies
gium. The centre of the country is,
ever, very high, mainly because of
chimney on it, and slopes down to a
at expanse of water, as they haven't
around to having the bathroom
rflow pipe fixed. The climate is
perate (remember that ninety per
t of Luxembourg is indoors) and the
al Flora is varied and interesting,
ecially on her favourite topic, the
8 five-cent blue triangular.

History

Luxembourg (now the coal-cellar of
modern country), was founded in
twelfth century by King John of
hemia, who wanted somewhere to
p the lawn-mower. It escaped most of
wars and pestilences that swept
rope in the subsequent eight
turies, often because the people
re out when they called, and is there-
e one of the most stable political and
nomic elements in the EEC: its
de-balance is always favourable (im-
ts come in at the back gate and
ve by the front door as exports).
xembourg is also the oldest ally of
anley Gibbons Ltd., although it is
bably most famous as the birthplace
Horace Batchelor.

NETHERLANDS

The People

Like the Germans, the Dutch fall into
two quite distinct physical types: the
small, corpulent, redfaced Edams, and
the thinner, paler, larger Goudas. As
one might expect of a race that evolved
underwater and subsisted entirely upon
cheese, the Dutch are somewhat single-
minded, conservative, resilient, and
thoughtful. Indeed, the sea informs
their entire culture: the bicycle, that
ubiquitous Dutch vehicle, was designed
to facilitate underwater travel, offering
least resistance to waves and weed, the
clog was introduced to weigh down the
feet and prevent drifting, and the meer-
schaum pipe, with its characteristic lid,
was designed expressly to exclude fish
and the larger plankton. And those who
would accuse the Dutch of overeating
would do well to reflect on the notorious
frangibility of dykes: it's no joke being
isolated atop a flooded windmill with
nothing to eat but passing tulips. You
have to get it while you can.

The Land

Strictly speaking, the land does not
exist: it is merely dehydrated sea, and
concern was originally expressed when
the EEC was first mooted that the Six
might suddenly turn into the Five after
a bad night. Many informed observers
believe that this fear is all that lies
behind the acceptance of Britain's
membership, i.e. we are a sort of First
Reserve in case Rain Stops Holland.
Nevertheless, it is interesting country,
sweeping up from the coastal plain into
the central massif, a two-foot high
ridge of attractive silt with fabulous
views of the sky, and down again to the
valleys, inches below. Apart from cheese
and tulips, the main product of the
country is advocaat, a drink made from
lawyers.

The History

Incensed by poor jokes about the Low
Countries, the Dutch, having emerged
from the sea, became an extremely
belligerent people, taking on Spain,
France, England, and Austria in quick
succession, a characteristic that has
almost entirely disappeared from the
modern Dutch temperament. It is now
found only among expatriate Dutchmen,
like Orangemen and Afrikaners.

ITALY

The People

The median Italian, according to the
latest figures of the Coren Intelligence
Unit, is a cowardly baritone who con-
sumes 78.3 kilometres of carbohydrates
a month and drives about in a car
slightly smaller than he is, looking for a
divorce. He is governed by a stable
conservative government, called the
Mafia, who operate an efficient police
force, called the Mafia, which is the
official arm of the judiciary, called the
Mafia. The Italians are an extremely
cultivated folk, and will often walk miles
to sell a tourist a copy of the Sistine
Chapel ceiling made entirely from sea-
shells. They invented the mandoline, a
kind of boudoir banjo shaped like a
woman's bottom, not surprisingly.

The Land

Italy is boot-shaped, for reasons lost in
the mists of geology. The South is
essentially agricultural, and admini-
stered by local land authorities, called
the Mafia; the North is industrial, and
run by tightly interlocked corporations,
called the Mafia. The largest Italian city
is New York, and is linked to the mainland by a highly specialised and efficient
communications system, called the
Mafia.

The History

Italy was originally called Rome, which
came to hold power over Europe by
moving into new areas every week or so
and threatening to lean on them if they
did not fork out tithe (L. *protectio*). It
was run by a series of Caesars (Eduardus
Gaius Robinsonius, Georgius Raftus,
Paulus Munius, etc.) who held sway
until the Renaissance, when Leonardo
invented the tank and the aeroplane,
and thus ushered in modern Italy (in
World War II, the Italians, ever brilliant,
possessed the only tank with a reverse
gear). In the 1920s, the Caesars re-
asserted themselves in their two main
linear branches, the Caponi and the
Mussolini, whose symbol was the fasces,
which signified "United We Stand," but
they didn't.

... And now, from two people who actually went into Europe last week ...

Report on the European Parliament

drawn up on behalf of the Punch editorial staff committee

Rapporteur: **Mr. Miles Kington**

Illustrateur: **Mr. Hewison**

THAT is how reports submitted to the European Parliament always begin. Reports are prepared by one of the dozen or so committees, who play a much larger part in the European Parliament than in ours because there is not very much else to discuss beside committee reports. These usually start with a brief resume of facts for those not acquainted with them. In this case, for instance, for those who have not the faintest idea what the European Parliament is.

1. (Reports make great use of numbered sections. This is a good idea, because it breaks up the page design and makes them look more interesting than they might otherwise appear.)

2. There are three main bodies concerned with the exercise of power in the European Community. The Commission is the European institution which initiates all policy governing the Community. The Council of Ministers represents the six national governments concerned; it is their job to tell the Commission that their proposals are too ambitious, too costly or too impractical, which they do by watering the proposals down, turning them down or ignoring them. The European Parliament has the responsibility of discussing these proposals in depth before they are ignored.

3. This is an extremely cynical view of affairs, with which many of the 142 members of the European Parliament would agree. They are all MP's at home, and nominated by their own parliaments. Britain would send 36 MP's.

4. European Parliament reports often vary the simple sequence of numbered paragraphs by introducing a new section in bold type.

Where it's at

5. It's at three different places. The administration is at Luxembourg, the committees meet in Brussels and the full sessions are held at Strasbourg. That explains why, when Mr. Hewison and I attended the full session at Strasbourg last week, the officials were all living out of tin trunks in temporary offices in the Maison de l'Europe.

6. The Maison de l'Europe, normally the home of the Council of Europe, looked to me like a fair-sized primary school and to Mr. Hewison like a Mussolini building. The committee has agreed to call it a Mussolini-type primary school, with added flagstaffs. Across the road is a large, rather beautiful park called the

The Parliament meets in Luxembourg as well as in Strasbourg, and everything and everybody moves. There's bound to be a mix-up some day.

Speeches are formal and stodgy—watch the simultaneous interpreters if you want a bit of liveliness.

Maison de L'Europe — Strasbourg
October 1971

Orangerie full of interesting trees. Some of them last week were dropping large green missiles which turned out to be walnuts.

Games that members can play

7. Among the things that members can do while not speaking are:

a) catch walnuts in the Orangerie;

b) watch the monkeys in the small Orangerie zoo catch the conkers which fall from the chestnut tree above their cage;

c) sit in the adjoining bar, as drinks are not actually served in the Assembly;

d) switch from one language to another on the simultaneous translation apparatus. This changes the character of a speech dramatically. When we listened to M. Armengaud, a French senator, he sounded cosy and homely in Dutch, seductive in Italian, rather doctrinaire in German and very no-nonsense in English. In French he was rather dry.

8. Green walnuts smell delicious straight off the tree, but by the time you've brought them home through English customs the aroma has vanished.

9. The members sit in a large semi-circle, called the hemicycle, arranged by political affiliation and not by nationality. As the president looks out from the focal point he sees to his left all the socialists, in the centre the Christian Democrats and on his right the liberals (who are not as liberal as they are here). On *their* right are the nineteen members of the European Democratic Union, who are all Gaullists but who think it sounds more proper to be called the EDU.

It is significant that of all the political groups the only one with a nationalist flavour should be French. There is a general feeling that the passing of De Gaulle has not meant the passing of French intrigue, French independence and French bloody-mindedness. For instance, you might expect that when English MP's come to Strasbourg after we enter Europe, the Tories would gravitate most naturally to the Christian Democrats. But the Gaullists have lost no time in making overtures; a few weeks ago there was a very friendly junket in Bordeaux for certain Tories. After all, the Gaullists will look much sillier in a bigger Parliament if they can get no-one to join them.

Another example of French obtuseness

10. The Parliament would dearly love to be elected directly by the people. It has spent ten years discussing ways and means of taking a step which could only mean more power, more respectability and more popular support. The French alone have resisted the idea.

11. The Parliament does not:

a) indulge in pageantry;

b) have fancy dress;

c) start sessions late in the day like Westminster, but at 9.30 am;

e) attract more than a mere handful of people to the public gallery.

12. In the Place de l'Université, there was a sharp rat-tat-tat as of gunfire and an elderly woman shrieked "Mon Dieu!". She was standing under a walnut tree. Miraculously, she emerged unstained.

13. There is a magazine called *Les Informations* which called its lead story last week: "London—Capital of Europe?". Britain, it said, is a sleeping giant who could still achieve great things. All it needs is a challenge. Such as Europe. They assume automatically that we are coming into Europe; what they are waiting to see is if it will wake us up.

In the middle of the magazine there was a bright advertising idea by a French construction firm—a 3-D model which sprang up as you opened it. At least, that was the idea; every time I opened it it got twisted or crumpled, and eventually it came away from its foundations. Miraculously, no-one was hurt.

There was another long feature on Britain in *France-Dimanche*. It was all about Princess Anne's secret love affair with a badly blown-up photo of a man; a messily retouched picture of the Queen is quoted as saying "One Tony in the family is enough!". I hope Mr. Heath will negotiate satisfactory terms for the export of scurrilous Royal stories.

14. Robert Pittomvils, the head of the interpreting service, has been with the Parliament since it began life in 1952 as the Assembly of the Coal and Steel

...EUROPE *WANTS* US .... EUROPE *NEEDS* US...

Mr. Heath makes the Nine o'clock News.

Strasbourg - Oct 1971.

Community (thus predating the Common Market). "The atmosphere has changed a lot. In the early days of the pioneers, when there were people like Spaak here, the speeches were full of fire and ideals and the bar was often empty. Now it is not so exciting but much more business-like."

English interpreters were provided right at the beginning for British observers; it seemed unfriendly to take them away again, so they are still there. As we were the only two British journalists in the place, there are obviously times when English is spilling out into the void like intergalactic messages of friendship.

"It's much harder to interpret speakers who are reading from a text, because they aren't thinking what they are saying and we can't enter their minds. And written language is so very different from spoken language. Of course it's easier not having interruptions. At least, there *are* interruptions, but the interrupters don't have their mikes on, so only a few people on the floor know what's happening."

15.   That's the difference. There is no cut and thrust, no sparking of ideas, as in an ordinary Parliament. It's difficult to cut and thrust in four official languages. Even if we bring the burden of another language, it is thought that Britain's arrival may enliven the scene (and bring one of the greatest parliamentary traditions to Europe). It may also make the place less bureaucratic. An information officer: "We have to get our memos signed by eight or nine people. Let us hope the British, with their trust in a man's word, can change all that." Hmm.

Hints for future British members in Strasbourg

16.   You should remember that:

a) In the place of its origin, the quiche lorraine is not a large tart, as it's properly made in England, but a small hors d'oeuvre. (You can, like Mr. Hewison, insist on having it as a main course and order two or three.)

b) If you lose your bus ticket, you pay a £1 fine on the spot. (You can, like Mr. Hewison, spend five minutes searching your clothing under the hard-boiled eye of a ticket inspector; he would obviously have liked nothing better than to whip out a gun and shoot him dead. Luckily, ticket inspectors are still for the moment unarmed in France.)

c) A cinema that advertises "un Western terrible" is showing a terrifying Western.

d) Strasbourg is a beautiful and friendly town. The only place we thought lacking in charm was a lane labelled "RUE PITTORESQUE".

e) The place is not stuffed with Scotsmen—it's just that there's a fashion for tartan caps with pompoms on top, which look silly on Frenchmen and wonderfully strange on Algerians.

f) The Common Market works in mysterious ways. While the Strasbourgeois are bombarded daily by walnuts, the food shops offer for sale "Walnuts—fresh from Italy!".

17.   From a report by Mr. Kriedemann: "The way in which the Council (of Ministers) has increasingly disregarded the repeated initiatives of the Commission instead of looking into them seriously,

must be seen as an indication that the governments of the member states have tacitly agreed to retain the greatest possible measure of independence over trade policy as a means of conducting a sovereign policy on traditional lines."

From a debate in 1960:
Mr. Smets (French): "Oh! Oh!"
President: "No bickering please! We are not yet a real Parliament." (Laughter).

18.   And until it gets power, it won't be. But, deprived of power, it has ideals to fall back on. Generally speaking, the role of the European Parliament is to counter-balance the narrow, naturally selfish motives of the Council and even of the Commission, one of whose members recently called the Parliament a farce. But it's only a farce if you think a call to duty and democratically expressed idealism a farce. If Europe has a conscience—something higher than a preoccupation with butter prices—then it is the European Parliament. If Europe is ever genuinely united, this Parliament, at present a brave travelling circus, may be the most important body in the Community. (And if Britain joins, London may wish to have a European body established here. The Parliament is the only one without a home.)

19.   Mr. Vredeling (last Tuesday morning):
"I am glad to see that in its latest policy on foreign aid, the Council has at last incorporated a few of the ideas which we have given so much thought to and fought for for so many years. I am only astounded that they did not bother to give any credit at all to the European Parliament."

"Well . . . let me put it this way. You know we've always worked as a team in this family? Well, daddy has put in for a transfer."

Sing a Song of Socialism

By LORD ARDWICK

The Tory Party enjoys every social advantage but one over Labour. It has no songs—in spite of its now having an occasional choirmaster as leader. It is most unlikely even at the Party conference that you will hear the sound of song emerging from the rooms where all those private dinner parties are held.

One feels there *ought* to be Tory songs—"Set the People Free," "He's the Best Prime Minister We Have," "The Lame Ducks Limped to Market." But the Tory officials assure me there is not and never has been a Tory Party Song Book.

The Liberals, too, are a party without song, though there are dim memories of the days when they sang:

God gave the Land to the People.

But that was in the days when Lloyd George was giving the Tories a taste of the Limehouse Blues and did he not come from what Tele Wele calls "The Land of Song?"

Labour is still a singing party and it is not only on Welsh night that the delegates convert the assembly rooms in Brighton's plush hotels into revolutionists' cellars, Methodist chapels and public house singing rooms. No left wing organisation, in fact, that I have ever flirted with can refrain from bursting into song. In the Thirties, the hunger marchers sang all the way from Jarrow to Downing Street:

We march from a stricken country,
From broken hill and vale
Where factory yards are empty
And rusty gear for sale.

So, in later years did the Aldermaston marchers. Even the stern matrons marching behind me in the Women's Lib demo last winter had a ribald version of *John Brown's Body*:

You can stuff your dirty underpants
and wash your filthy socks,
When the day of Liberation dawns.

The Labour Party is the only one to have an official song book—words and music. Of course it starts with Jim Connell's *The Red Flag* and gives all five verses—though the first and last verses only are sung at the wind-up of the party conference. Of course the British Labour Party itself has no revolutionary traditions or aspirations, and the hymn has been an embarrassment to our gentle social democrats for many years. But it has to be maintained as a kind of musical Clause IV. The fourth is the juiciest of the unknown verses:

> It suits to-day the wealth and base,
> Whose minds are fixed on pelf and place
> To cringe before the rich man's frown,
> And haul the sacred emblem down.

Whom can they be thinking of? But, of course, the Labour Party—as Morgan Philips used to say—is more Methodist than Marxist.

After *The Red Flag* in the song book comes Edward Carpenter's noble hymn:

> England, arise! the long, long night is over,
> Faint in the East, behold the dawn appear.

And though the Communist *International* comes next, it is immediately followed by *Jerusalem* and the 23rd psalm to the setting of *Crimond*. And on page seven there is the mighty *Cwm Rhondda*, hot from the chapels in the valley and the popular side of Cardiff Arms Park. The *Labour Party Song Book* gives the words in English and Welsh.

"He's really been a good son to us, your honour —we hardly ever see him."

It is this kind of thing which used to upset Lenin and today still foxes anti-clerical European socialist parties. Even with the comradely relations which will be strengthened when we are in the Common Market, I cannot imagine the most revisionist French and German social democrats joining in:

> Guide me, O Thou Great Jehovah!
> Pilgrim thro' this barren land.

In the Thirties, when many of us cautiously fellow-travelled with the Communists, we sang stronger stuff in what Nye Bevan used to describe as "the cringeing minor keys" beloved of oppressed nations.

> A man is only human
> He must eat before he can think
> Fine words are only empty air
> And not his meat and drink.
> So Left, Right, Left
> So Left, Right, Left.
> There's a place comrades for you
> March with us in the workers' united front
> For you are a worker too.

Mr. Harold Lever and I can still render this with feeling. Another song which appealed to those of us intoxicated by the Left Book Club's *Military Strength of the Powers* with its praise for the Red Army was:

> Fly higher, and higher, and higher,
> Our emblem the Soviet Star.
> When ev'ry propeller is roaring
>   "Red Front!"
> Defending the U.S.S.R.

The words "Red Front" were not sung, but shouted with abandon in the style of the Red Army choir.

The Communist Party has no song book today. If you want to consult the old *Left Song Book*, you have to go to Marx Memorial House in Clerkenwell. And the engaging permissive satires of the Fabian Society are guarded not in Dartmouth Street, but in the archives lodged at Nuffield College, Oxford.

The Communist Party, asked for their songs, will today refer you to the Workers Music Association in W.11. For 13 new pence you can have *The Jacket Makers' Song* from North Vietnam by Xuan Hong. The words are less than stirring:

Burnt by sun and soaked by rain
Freedom fighters still stand firm.
We make jackets out of cloth
Jackets for our men to keep them warm.

Refrain:

Fighters, you are stubborn, strong;
All I can give you, I will give.
You brothers speed up the work
For those who fight that we may live.

One fears that, like the *Thoughts of Chairman Mao*, the opus may have suffered in translation.

Of course there are some songs that are local and topical, like *Landlord's Song*, which claims:

We don't take coloureds, we don't take kids,
We don't take Irish, Wops or Yids;
Get your own blankets, extra for a sheet,
The room dries out if you use enough heat.

The best thing this organisation does is a collection of industrial folk ballads edited by Ewan McColl. One of them is of the Gresford pit disaster (245 dead) which I covered as a young reporter and noted the bitterness which produced a verse like this:

The Lord Mayor of London's collecting
To help both the children and wives
The owners have sent some white lilies
To pay for the colliers' lives.

Joan Littlewood or somebody should now give us "O What a Lovely Class War." There's as much anguish, fun and mockery in Labour's songs as there was in those of World War I. And they are not all that different.

"You'd think a big police force like ours wouldn't need help with their enquiries."

A Chinese Guide to
BASIC ENGLISH

Written English, like Chinese, is based on a series of pictograms. Originally they were all directly representational, though many have changed greatly over the centuries. Here are some of the most common ones a Chinese visitor may expect to find

Underground Railway
Literally: the - line - that - lies - straight - is - not - always - as - quick - as - the - way - round. From an old British proverb, "The wind that springs up no man knows from where is more to be trusted than the Holborn Kingsway escalators."

An Export
The - thing - that - works - till - spare - parts - are - needed. The pictogram is an idealised version of one of the first winners of the Queen's Award for Industry, a machine for opening self-sealing envelopes.

A Train
Self-explanatory symbol: the-one-coming-will-not - be - here - for - a - long -time - and - the - one - about-to-go-has-already-gone.

The Sea
A pictogram invented by the legendary sailor, Chi Chester. Returning from his most famous voyage, he claimed to have seen such marvels across the ocean as a Harris Tweed suit thirty years old with its creases still intact, and a woollen sock which went fifty days without washing.

A Serious Newspaper
Literally, that - which - thinks - it - knows - all - it - needs-to-know. It is the custom for some elderly British mandarins or lords to receive reports from all over the world, which they pretend to attach great importance to; in fact, they are much more interested in contentious letters from elderly acquaintances.

A Popular Newspaper
This symbol represents reverence for the old-fashioned members of the community. Many British 'mandarins and lords are convinced that unless traditional values are upheld, the country will go to the dogs, and they go to extreme lengths to promote them.

Peace
The British have always dreamed of a weapon that would put an end to war. This pictogram is based on the design for a rocket which, when launched, would scatter paper flowers and butterflies ·across the world. Sadly, it never worked.

A Perfect Meal
British cooking is one of the great arts of the world, but a meal can easily be spoilt by a customer passing a dud cheque or simply running out in the street without paying. Hence this symbol, literally: crispy-pound- note-him-fulfil-all-human-aspiration.

A Factory Product
At one time, any object which enjoyed Imperial approval at the British court was singled out for special honour, but so many members of the royal household endorsed so many products that the symbol now means only that the firm is not yet bankrupt. The design is based on a typical Victorian inkwell.

A Literary Agent

When a British writer wants a book published, he takes it to a certain kind of book-lover who will sell it to a publisher on condition the author gets some of the money. Literally: Your-writings - are - as - precious - as - the - moon - and - I-intend-to-get-the-first-quarter.

A Lost Suitcase

Self-explanatory symbol. Your - luggage - has - sprouted - wings - and - flown - by - itself - to - Frankfurt.

An Old Car

Literally: "the thing which supports the other two things is worn out and will cost much gold to replace."

Roast Peasant

One of the rarest of British delicacies. It is prepared by erecting huge (80 ft high) electric heaters in a field, and waiting for someone to walk into them.

Happiness

It is impossible to transcribe the British concept of happiness. Roughly, it means beauty-plus-usefulness-plus-gentleness-plus-a-reasonable-profit-margin. The symbol represents centuries of philosophical evolution and can easily be attached to the livingroom wall with two $\frac{3}{8}$" grummet swizzle screws.

Wisdom

The three great symbols of wisdom, these three birds were supposed to be all-seeing, all-knowing. An old legend has it that if you asked the pelican the time, he would reply with a three-hour lecture on the economics of Aramaic basketwear.

Doors

For some inscrutable reason, the British, have always thought of doors as being either male or female. It is not known exactly how they distinguish between a male and female door.

Bad News

The British, who hate being the personal bearers of bad news, prefer to send it in a dull brown envelope. The crown is a propitiatory symbol, meaning may - your - contribution - be - melted - down - into - something - useful - for - the - royal - yacht.

Poetry

Poetry, in Britain, is something more than just words set prettily on a page (which, in fact, they rarely read). It is a state of mind; it is usually reached after about five pints at which point they feel that anything they say *is* poetry. This is sometimes called the Irish fallacy.

A Grand Hotel

There is nothing quite like a great British hotel, or boarding-house for business conferences. The pictogram signifies the-facade-is-brilliantly-lit-at-all-times-to-keep-you-awake.

The Simple Life

There is nothing the British love more than returning to the countryside for the basic essentials. The items depicted in the symbol are not necessarily the most basic, but they are easier to depict than, say, the plastic tomato sauce-holder, the filter stub or the dead chip.

(This symbol has been temporarily withdrawn from the English language pending certain alterations. We hope to have it back on the page fairly soon.)

Fair Stood the Wind for France

in which ALAN COREN swims the Channel in style

"Sorry, we forgot the knife—try sticking a glucose tablet up its nose."

Ninety-six years ago, Captain Matthew Webb became the first man to swim the English Channel, and ended up on matchboxes in his underwear. Such is the nature, such it was bound to be, of cross-Channel immortality: it is an activity without style, without panache, without flair of any kind. It is a feat as ploddy and grotesque in its success as in its failure: the man who swims it, after five years of slogging to and fro in the public baths, hobbles up the French or English pebbles in his puffy feet, dropping such tiny blobs of greasy pollution as the waves have left him, and is immediately forgotten; the man who fails is hauled aboard, cramped rigid or lolly-cold, and bloated on cocoa, is beached like a waning cod. There are also women who become involved in this oleaginous nightmare; but of their exposure and indignity I am too gallant a soul even to speak.

It came to me, a week or so ago and at the beginning of what aquabuffs are pleased to call The Channel Season (as if the thing shared the cool nobility of grouse or oysters), that there was, surely, no need for all the dreary seriousness with which this aquatic farce is invested. Why was the Channel always swum (or, alternatively, unswum) by these dedicated monkish stoics who spent the best years of their lives in churning up ten miles of local chlorine a day and spooning down glucose in preparation for the great fiasco? Why could the Channel not attract its playboy sportsmen, its dashing rogues, fighting heroes with a bird on either arm and Bollinger under the belt?

So I phoned the Channel Swimming Association.

"I'm afraid he's out," said the Channel Swimming Association's wife. "Shall I send you the forms?"

"Forms?" I said. I may have allowed a quizzical boyish smile to ripple the steely ridge of my upper lip. "I am not applying for a rent rebate, madame. I wish to swim to France."

90

"You'll have to fill in the forms," she said, "and include requisite fee. Eight pounds one-way, twelve pounds two-way, sixteen pounds three-way."

"Three-way?"

"The fee," she said, unfazed, "does not, of course, include vellum certificate ratifying successful swim, which is available for a further eight pounds from the Secretary."

"No doubt," I murmured, "there is also a blazer badge?"

"Wire, eight pounds, cloth, fifty new pence," said the Channel Swimming Association's wife. "And/or tie at 1.25 pounds."

"I don't want all that," I said, "I wish merely to drive down to Dover, hand my valuables to my chauffeur, and set out at a fast clip for le Continong. Is this too much to ask?"

"It wouldn't be ratified," she said, "unless you had an accredited observer, cost of same, including boat, being approximately one hundred pounds."

"I don't want it ratified," I said.

There was a sibilant inhalation in the earpiece.

"But suppose you broke the record?" she said, shocked.

"That alone," I said softly, "would be ample reward. I am not a man, madame, to flaunt my prowess at the world via twenty-five bobsworth of tie. All I require from you is the information of where to start the swim, and where to acquire the grease used, I believe, on such occasions."

"I'm afraid I can't help you," she said stiffly. "Swimmers are not allowed any assistance of that nature."

"Then how may I find out?" I enquired.

"You could contact a known Channel swimmer," she said, making the hero sound like someone with three previous convictions. "Police Constable Frayne at Canterbury police station might help you. I couldn't promise."

"He might be up the swimming-baths," said the station-sergeant, when I finally got through to Canterbury nick. "If he's not here, he's there."

That's dedication for you. A life so simply divided. I had a vision of the sodden helmet, just visible as he made his hundredth kick-turn of the morning and started back towards the shallow end. PC Frayne, however, turned out to be on the premises. I filled him in.

"When were you thinking of going?" he asked.

"Today," I said. "The sun's out, and the *Times* says Channel smooth."

"You're not having me on, I hope?"

"No," I said. "Why?"

"Well, you've missed the tide, for one thing. Hang on, I've got a tidal chart in my pocket. Here we are, July 2, high tide at Dover 6.36 am. You should have been away at 7.30 sharp."

If there's one thing I've learned in life, it's that you don't treat frivolously a copper who carries tidal charts about his person. Needless to say, I had no intention of bothering with such trivia as tides.

"Well, can you tell me where to get grease?" I said.

"What you want is a compound of two parts lanoline to one part Vaseline," he said. "The Boots at Dover does it. And don't forget your roller-towel."

"I'm sorry?"

"You don't know much about Channel swim-

ming, do you?" said PC Frayne, with a perception that'll take him into the CID in no time, if I'm any judge. "There you are, ten miles out, covered in grease, and you cramp up: now, how're they going to get you aboard the escort boat? You'll go through their fingers like an eel. What you need is a roller towel. First sign of trouble, they chuck it out, you loop the end under your shoulders, they haul you in, no problem. Are you fit?"

I debated briefly whether or not to inform him that I had spent the previous night drinking Jack Daniels and drawing unsuccessfully to inside straights until the money ran out at four am, and decided against. I stubbed out my twelfth cigarette of the morning.

"As a fiddle," I said.

"Good luck," he said.

I took my bikini and passport from the office drawer in which they had been waiting patiently for the chance of stardom, and strolled down the corridor to select a couple of citizens for the escort boat. I found Miles Kington and Geoffrey Dickinson leaning industriously against the art room wall; they did not look much like oarsmen or men skilled in the arcane art of roller-towel pitching, but they were all I had. Also, there was the advantage that they were in no position to steal my thunder, should pictures of the successful swim reach the world's front pages: Kington is not unattractive, in a pale dishevelled way, but abhors publicity; Dickinson, on the other hand, is greedy for fame, but horrible to look upon, except in his own drawings of himself, where his inaccuracy infects the whole to the point of libelling some of the best-looking humorous writers in the world.

"We're going to Dover," I said.

They woke, briefly, and murmured something pithy.

"On expenses," I said.

They were waiting in the garage when I got out of the lift.

We chose a blue Mercedes convertible for the trip, since style was the essence and since, it being a time of Common Market fervour, it seemed an ideal springboard for my personal entry into Europe. Silkily, the hood down and the boot full of roller-towels and champagne, I aimed the three-pointed star in the general direction of Dover and slipped the clutch.

The toughest part of any Channel swim is undoubtedly the bit between the Elephant and Castle and New Cross: it took us an hour to clear London and get on the wrong road to Dover. Noon passed; lunch loomed.

"We shall eat," said Kington, who had arrogated to himself the role of technical adviser

"All in favour of these Channel swims—gives us a chance to meet people from abroad."

92

"I'm an armaments manufacturer and it seems to me that you have an ideal spot here to start a guerilla war."

(Dickinson having been driven into a squat stupor by the wealth of female hitchhikers on the A20), "at the Wyf of Bath in Wye. Its style is beyond taint."

We turned up there two hours later, having followed Dickinson's meticulous navigation, and sank gratefully into a cool magnum of Moet & Chandon, a secret preparation knocked up by those two matchless chemists which I heartily recommend to all aspiring Channel swimmers. After a couple of bottles, you feel you could tackle Cape Horn in a Force Ten gale, at the backstroke. I helped it down with vitality-giving iced walnut soup, lobster à l'armoricaine, elderflower sorbet, and a brie that dissolved on the palate like tangy cream. Ordering another quart of champagne seemed unwise, so I settled for a Lafitte you could stand a fork in: I am no Cyril Ray, but even I could tell it had a thick edge over glucose tablets.

The escort team helped me to the car, and propped me behind the wheel. I thought for a while, selected first gear, and kept it most of the way to Dover; with four to choose from, I was in no shape to make complex decisions.

"*Twelve* pounds of Vaseline?" said the Boots assistant.

Dickinson breathed on her, and she sent for the manager.

"Swimming the Channel," I explained to his suit. "Need grease."

"We *can* prepare the requisite compound," said the manager, "but we need twenty-four hours. The lanoline has to be heated and dropped gradually into the Vaseline. Have you brought a bucket?"

I shook my head, and steadied myself on Kington, against the pain.

"We'll just take the Vaseline," I said. "And a tin of glucose."

The female assistant wrapped it solicitously.

"You know you've missed the tide?" she said.

They know their Channel down there, I'll say that for them.

"I do not give a tide for figs, madame!" I cried, just failing to snap my fingers, and strode nobly into the glass door.

It did not take long for a small suspicious crowd to collect at the beach, the sort of people

93

who, narrow as they are, find it somehow curious to see three drunks fall out of a gigantic car carrying a suitcase, a barrel of Vaseline, an armful of booze, and a roller towel. Unfortunately, the last item fell as we stepped onto the shingle, and unrolled itself down thirty yards of beach and into the sea, like a ceremonial carpet. On hands and knees, we rolled it up again. Small boys threw stones. I changed beneath my bathrobe with all the deft grace of an ox executing the pas-de-deux, while matrons hid their eyes, and turned to find Kington gone. Dickinson was lying face down on a broken deck-chair. I woke him.

"Where's Kington?" I said.

Posy

"This is my best suit," said Dickinson. He picked a flake of choc-ice from his lapel, and was about to weep when Kington returned with a gnarled thing in tow. They were carrying four oars of assorted lengths between them.

"It's a pound an hour," said the boatman, "and no standing up."

And it was then, glancing at the listing hulk, that I caught my first sight of the Channel: it was grey-brown beneath an ochre scum, in which bobbed a villainous stew of broken bottles, old beer-cans, lolly-sticks, tar, newspaper and an inordinate number of items that had, if lexicography is to be believed, been posted in France. Jellyfish lolled a yard offshore, malevolently.

It was no place for a gentleman. Indeed, there was only one way, in such evil circumstances, to behave with anything approaching style.

"Kington," I said, summoning natural authority with ease, "get in."

I turned to the gawping crowd.

"My man," I explained, "will swim it for me."

And, for a hundred yards or so, he did. The trouble was that the escort boat not only had four unmatched oars, it also had only three rowlocks, and Dickinson sozzled at the stern. In consequence of which, Kington had to keep stopping to give his support boat time to catch up. A natural leader, I came to the swift conclusion that the reason why the Channel had never been swum with style was, quite simply, because it is a length of alien muck with which no person of *ton* could possibly associate himself. We looped the roller-towel around the latest challenger, and wound him aboard; and, a hundred yards or so up the coast, well away from the cynics, we beached our seeping tub, and dismounted. Our champagne was warm as the afternoon, and there was but one course of action. Like pale immigrants, we crunched up the beach with our luggage, crawled onto the promenade, and staggered towards the nearest pub.

We found it in East Cliff. With incredible aptness, given our feelings at the time, it was called The First And Last. It was a coincidence better than I could ever have dreamed of. It had style.

Dressed to Kill

QUENTIN BLAKE inspects
the fashionable troops
on the Mediterranean front

"And this is Daddy."

"*Doin' all right for a feller who made his money out of goldfish for jam-jars, eh!*"

Sam Hinchcliffe at Ascot

by BILL TIDY

"*What do you think, luv? A magnum for a chip's not a bad offer!*"

"*Ah say, luv. Lend my missus your hat!*"

"*We don't want trouble, Archie. Her Majesty says it's OK.*"

"*Owns pigeons!*"

THE BRIEN PAPERS

The following article by
ALAN BRIEN,
containing many hitherto
undisclosed facts, has
come into our hands. We
consider it in the national
interest to publish it now

The Pentagon Papers, the Anderson Papers . . . everybody seems to be publishing everybody else's dirty documents. Ministers of state and heads of departments all over the world must be suffering an uneasy flutter in the pits of their stomachs each time they dictate a memorandum or initial an order in council for fear it will appear in the press a week later. They call for stricter security precautions, more stringent penalties for leaking, judicial injunctions against editors. But the remedy is much simpler—print every piece of paper which passes from every out-tray to in-tray among their bureaucrats every day, load them into vans and dump them in the lobbies of every newspaper, and the muckrakers would be buried alive in an avalanche of verbiage. The safest place for a secret is in an official handout, or a White Paper.

I myself have never had a big hang-up about privacy. I'll read any friend's diary, letters, address-book, bills, bank statements, advertising circulars, even the small print on their sauce bottles, though I sometimes have to draw a line at their novels. The point is that what I read must be something they might not want me to read. Over the years, those around me have learned that no handbag, briefcase, bottom drawer, inside pocket or open desk is safe from my obsessive prying. It's a kind of disease, I realise, like kleptomania or claustrophobia.

Unfortunately for me, it rarely attracts the same sympathy and understanding for the sufferer. And I can foresee the day when I shall have to sit in court and hear myself described as a journalist, going through a difficult age, subject to hot flushes, under pressure from the Inland Revenue, who realises now that he ought not to have downed a second light ale while carrying on taking the pills, but is willing to submit to treatment.

The drive for me is almost automatic. I am the man next to you on the tube who leans over to race your eyes down the columns of the evening

paper even though I have the same edition in my pocket. I always gravitate to your side of the desk, turn over the postcards on your mantelpiece, read the figures on your cheque backwards on the blotting paper, study the notices on the board in your office corridor. I'll sit for hours tuned in to a crossed line while two matrons discuss the best route from Aldgate to Golders Green, or linger until the ice crusts over on my coffee while three businessmen at the next table try to recall the name of the tall fair girl who is the receptionist at Midland Hotel in Manchester.

In the grip of my mania, I become boredom-proof. I would be willing to spend a bank holiday weekend burgling the Public Records Office, to be assistant censor of children's thank-you letters to Santa Claus c/o the GPO, relief graffiti-eraser in the washroom of the College of Cardinals. With my failing eye-sight and lousy memory, I don't expect any rewards from my research.

It is the process I enjoy, not what can be purchased with the end product, the medium not the message. Somewhere in my de-formative years, I developed this desire to be an extra feed-box on other people's wiring diagrams, the third carbon in anybody's correspondence file, the spy who stayed out in the cold watching the lighted window of the empty room.

I should be embarrassed if I actually stumbled across state secrets, commercial plots, private confessions, political scandals, or material for *Private Eye* or *Forum* magazines. I merely hope to be reassured that the rest of humanity are as open a book, and with as little chance of finding a publisher, as I am. I hanker for a lovely empty existence, where I have nothing to do and I can put it off until tomorrow.

In so far as there are any engagements in my diary, I only entered them there because I thought 1972 would never come, and now I wish somebody else would keep them. When the telephone rings, not only would I be highly flattered to believe it was being tapped, but I would be grateful if the tapper cut in first to explain to the caller that I had gone to Tibet for the

"Where shall I leave the horse?"

rest of the year. Every unopened envelope takes on to me the aspect of an unexploded bomb, and I would be willing to pay a small de-fusing fee to the postman if he would shout a quick precis through the letter-box before depositing them on the doormat. Any visitor is welcome to examine the Brien Papers, I certainly don't intend to.

Sometimes, by accident, I do sneak a look at my own documents and find that I can make even less sense of them than I would of yours. Trained snoopers can build up a whole character pattern from a laundry list, they say—what sort of person went through a month sending in 25 socks, and only one shirt, to be washed? Why do I have these bills from restaurants I swear I have never entered—surely if I had ever had tea at the Ritz in Neasden I would have remembered. Dare I ever ring these numbers of Ted and Bob and Carol and Alice preserved on the backs of cigarette packets, invariably of brands I do not smoke? For what article for what paper could I have preserved these cuttings about the incidence of head colds in Alaska, the amount of permitted preservative in Italian sausage, the number of times the word "hallelujah" appears in the New Testament? Who sent me the manuscript of a play in which Act One is set in "10,000 BC" and Act Two "Ten minutes later"? Whatever happened to the money for those BBC contracts, for half of which I seem to have signed and sent back the top copy and the other half the second copy?

The Brien Papers seem to be mainly by, from, and about other people, or at best a me I do not recognise. Whatever they are, there are a lot of them, filling up all the suitcases I thought were empty, carpeting the floors and climbing up the walls of any room I have not entered for a couple of days. I wish some PhD with a life-time on his hands, or even some rag-and-bone man with room on his cart, would carry them off when my back is turned, which is most of the decade. I have enough to do poking my nose into other people's business without trying to run a muniment room and department of archives on myself.

Stratford is Real Cool, Man

Entirely Surrounded by Dames of America, E. S. TURNER tours The Stratford Circuit

"You will notice there are no billboards," said the silver-haired guide, as the silver-haired driver coaxed his cargo of silver-haired American ladies along the road to Stratford-upon-Avon. Nobody rose to this, not even when we passed the odd billboard.

We were a bleached-out lot, to be sure, with the notable exception of two identical girl twins, aged about nineteen. Piquant as the Doublemint doxies, they wore the same clothes, the same hair slides, with the same number of hairs trapped under each slide; and they moved with the calm grace of those who know the world is watching.

I had been assigned to the London-Stratford tour as a corrective to two years globe-trotting. What could be more deflationary, and at the same time educative, than a two-day foray into the Shakespeare Country, listening to overseas visitors expressing wonder at speedwells, or saying things like, "Walter, what was the name of that place where you got the trots?" As it happened, there were only two Walters in the coach; the others toiled in distant skyscrapers, or lay in distant graves.

At the first coffee-stop, in a fifteenth century inn at Tetsworth, the conversation turned naturally enough to Siberia. Had I ever stopped over at Irkutsk? Regretfully, I said no. The lady who had done so said she had worn padded pyjamas and advised me to do the same. It turned out that we had both been to Alma-Ata, but she had been there when all the apple trees were in bloom.

The guide, who was spare and a little tight-faced, spoke into his microphone in slow,

measured terms. If we did not enjoy ourselves, he warned us, it would be our own fault. He said this as we neared the Hoover factory ("You ladies have to thank them for a lot"). England, he told us, contained far more open country than most Americans imagined. For our benefit, he identified hawthorn, chestnut, laburnum, lilac, gorse.

The countryside was so fresh and virginal that it was no grave hardship to take one's eyes off the twins. I wanted to tell the lady with the padded pyjamas that Buckinghamshire was not less beautiful than the Valley of Roses, in Bulgaria, where I had been a couple of weeks before; but she would probably have countered by saying it was even finer than Kashmir two days ago. If any of us had doubts whether the countryside was beautiful, the guide soon dispelled them. Perhaps, on the Stratford Circuit, there should be a quotation from the Bard mounted above the guide's head:

> *Beauty itself doth of itself persuade*
> *The eyes of men without an orator.*

In Oxford a cluster of embarrassed youths were tickling the Town Hall with white wands, but the guide forebore to comment on this indelicacy. A passenger explained to her companion that they were beating the bounds, just one of those things. We went straight to Christ Church College and entered the great hall, after passing two huge signs saying it was closed. Shining spoons were being laid out on shining tables, but nobody seemed to resent us.

Pausing under a portrait inscribed "Charles Lutwidge Dodgson," the guide asked, "Does anybody know who this is?" No one spoke. The position of an Englishman on a tour of his own country is a sensitive one. Was I to risk a charge of showing off, and say, "Lewis Carroll?" Eventually I did so and was cordially congratulated. One of the group continued to be puzzled by the presence of a native; she thought I was there to see that people did not bounce about on historic chairs.

In Christ Church Hall we laughed dutifully at the story of the undergraduate who was the victim of a prank when his turn came to read out grace. Knowing nothing of Latin, he recited a substituted text which was highly critical of the food.

The guide had already educated us in Oxford jargon and told us that anyone who said "I *left* Oxford in such-and-such a year" was a phoney. He begged us not to talk of teachers and classes, but one of the Walters had to be rebuked for doing so. The other Walter took copious notes all the time. So did one or two of the ladies. What do Americans do with all these notes back home?

We had now done Oxford, apart from a glance at the Martyrs' Memorial. Lunch awaited us at Woodstock, where the Yorkshire pudding was not quite of the standard to set before heavenly twins. Of Blenheim Palace we saw but a fleeting, distant prospect. Then the guide stopped the coach and became a little mysterious. "Follow me," he said, and headed up an insignificant lane. It brought us to the churchyard where the Churchills lie. Propped against each stone adjoining Sir Winston's grave was a hand-lettered card saying "Son," "Father," "Mother," "Cousin" and so on. Well, Bladon in some measure made up for skirting Stoke Poges without stopping and without comment.

By way of the Cotswolds, with occasional photo calls, we reached Stratford and went straight to Holy Trinity Church where the poet lies. It contained nearly as many Americans as the Sistine Chapel. Near the door the paperbacks for sale included: *The Gospel According To Peanuts; God Is For Real, Man; God Is Beautiful, Man; Treat Me Cool, Lord; The Way I See It*, by Cliff Richard; and *Family Planning and Christian Marriage*. "That Peanuts book is real good," somebody said.

Not included in the tour was the Louis Tussaud Shakespearean Waxworks, which by a happy coincidence had opened that very day. For 20 pence one can see Marianne Faithfull, Tommy Steele, the Burtons and other eminent Shakespeareans in scenes from the plays; and there is a splendid record of the witches gibbering at Macbeth.

The play in the Memorial Theatre that evening was *Twelfth Night*. House full, of course. Some believe the only way to get a ticket to this theatre is to book on a sightseeing tour. The lady on my right had been brought up on the Shakespearean productions of Ashland, Oregon, which is the Shakespeare Capital of the West and runs a three-months outdoor season.

What did they think of *Twelfth Night?* Why, what everybody thinks of it, except the critics. A silly play, really, with siblings unable to recognise each other; but marvellously done. A bit kinky? Yeah, I'll say.

Next morning we swept into Anne Hathaway's Cottage, much of it recently rebuilt after a jilted swain tried to burn it down. You get guys like that everywhere, of course. An elderly lady from Westchester looked disapprovingly at some hemlock in the garden. "You know, this is a weed in the United States," she said. She was anxious to check some information on plants with the guide, but confessed, "I hate to ask him because he likes to think you remember everything he says."

In the Birthplace we were addressed by an authority who had actually talked to descendants of Shakespeare's sister. There was time to visit the tartan shop and buy Shakespeare humbugs. Then we took off for Warwick Castle, where the executioner's mask reminded somebody of a relative in Indiana. There was general agreement that it had been a bit of a liberty to ask Reynolds to extend that portrait by Van Dyck, especially when it meant painting such a dull expanse of skirt. The butler-like Castle guide had his quiet little jokes; about George III, whom some of you may have heard of, and Anne Boleyn, who did not die of ill-health. "There must be a powder room in the Castle," said somebody. There was.

Nobody complained that the great trees in the grounds were regarded as weeds in Texas. The hit of the tour was the peacocks, as proud, well-groomed and expansive as one can find in Britain. No wonder Warwick is near the top of the stately homes league; if it were any more romantic it would be unbearable.

On the resumed journey the guide became less tight-faced. He had told us stories about William Penn, Benjamin Disraeli and Winston Churchill; now he told us stories about Sctosmen and Irishmen. Only once had he to halt his discourse to say, "Anybody want the mike?" The chatterers then subsided. It happens on every trip; some tourists just don't know their place.

Long before Banbury all was forgiven and the atmosphere was verging on the Butlinesque. We were asked to recite, all together, the nursery rhyme relevant to the town, and we did so. The driver, a jolly version of Edward Heath, had endured a good many jokes about sleeping at the wheel. For some time he had been conducting a public courtship of the old lady from Westchester. Eventually she said, in the hearing of all, "I want you to know there are walls and hedges and fields and ditches between you and me." It raised a bigger laugh than the clown had done in *Twelfth Night.*

At one point somebody asked the driver about Scotland. It was delightfully uncrowded, he said; and the only thing that could ruin it would be a lot of hotels with private bathrooms. The silver-haired ladies who went along with this possibly did so more from politeness than conviction. There were some notable critics of plumbing among them.

By way of battery farms and bomber bases we came to Sulgrave Manor, ancestral home of the Washingtons, where Old Glory flew from a flag-staff and a sign paid tribute to the public spirit of the Colonial Dames of America. In a window we saw a coat of arms containing stars and stripes, which may or may not have inspired the flag. There is a fascinating kitchen, full of better mousetraps, and gadgets for ironing a collar with the aid of a red-hot poker, and a melodious alarm clock which would have roused George himself from dreams of sedition if only he had lived there.

And that was it, except for a few more funny stories, and an assurance that free houses were no more free than public schools were public. "Have you all enjoyed yourselves?" asked the guide, and the chorus was "We sure have." Shortly afterwards the guide said he had been asked whether it was permissible to give tips. "Yes," he ruled, not too austerely, "if you have enjoyed yourselves it is quite permissible to tip." What was it the man said in *Coriolanus?* "Make them be strong and ready for this hint . . ."

And the twins? As they emerged into Holborn they continued to gladden the eyes of men, without an orator.

"Say—it's really great to be invited into a typical English home."

The ABC of Tourist Britain

OMLETS: These are what the waiter will bring if American visitors do not learn to say "Omelettes."

BARBER: A vendor of contraceptives, who also cuts hair.

CONVERSAZIONE: Like a cocktail party, but with less to drink. Always take a small barrel of beer with you.

DRUGS: If an Englishman has a glazed look in his eyes and tries to walk right through you, do not assume he is drugged; it may be his normal condition.

ELIOT, T. S., COUNTRY, THE: All visitors want to know where it is. Ask any taxi driver.

FOLLIES: Buildings erected by rich men for no apparent purpose, or as conversation pieces; e.g. Centre Point, an unoccupied skyscraper in London.

GEAR: Dress which is better suited to the nursery, the rodeo, the lamaserie or the brothel is known as Gear.

HOGMANAY: Misleadingly described by the late Evelyn Waugh as "people being sick on the pavement in Glasgow." The alert traveller will find that Hogmanay is practised in almost all communities, especially on Friday and Saturday nights.

ICEBERGS: Britain is full of icebergs, but only the tips are visible. They all contain the seeds of national decay.

JABBER: Visitors should try not to. If they pronounce their own language loudly and clearly the British will understand them.

KITCHENER, LORD: A distinguished British soldier who is remembered only through his valet.

LAVATORIES: The non-pedestal, hole-in-the-floor type with foot treads is gradually being installed at British airports, to bring Britain into line with European standards. Meanwhile visitors should do their best to use the traditional British kind.

MOTELS: These are both scarce and dear. Try a four-star hotel, unless you *enjoy* hearing an E-type revved up outside your door at four am.

NORTH OF ENGLAND: Spawning-ground of the chip-on-shoulder accents and ingenious mispronunciations now favoured in domestic broadcasting. Foreigners who wish to hear correct English should stay at home and listen to the BBC Overseas Service.

OUTBACK, THE: See North of England.

POLICEMAN: One who would rather raid a pornographer than fish a corpse out of the river.

QUEUES: The British prefer to shuffle along behind each other, instead of bumping and boring. A very long shuffling queue does not necessarily lead to the Heath Mausoleum.

RUBBING, BRASS: A few churches still remain open so that visitors, for a suitable fee, may make rubbings of saints' faces for use in coffee bars and love nests.

STOCK CAR RACING: To be seen on London's North and South Circular Roads daily, 8 am to 10 am and 4.30 pm to 6.0 pm.

THERMOMETERS: Available from souvenir shops. Simply detach the toy Guardsman and the instrument is ready for use.

UNDERGROUND, LONDON: A self-governing Commonwealth community established in catacombs under London, where train-cancelling has been elevated to a way of life.

VICES, ENGLISH: Colonising, litter-strewing, baby battering, puritanism, litter-strewing, perfidy, litter-strewing.

WORLD THEATRE SEASON: An annual feast of abstruse polyglot entertainment imported from illiberal countries. The most successful show to date is India's long-running "Oh, Calcutta!"

XENOPHOBIA: The feeling of impotent rage which besets an Englishman when he has to ask a Nigerian the way to Hackney Wick.

YOB: Any hooligan not on the strength of a university; one who wrecks Chinese restaurants in preference to Greek.

ZEE: The sound made by Americans trying to say "Zed" or by Frenchmen trying to say "The."

"... and we musn't forget purchase tax, must we?"

"It smells absolutely delicious."

SPANKING NEW AND A SNIP AT THE PRICE

Fully guaranteed by
GRAHAM

"Speedometer . . . rev. counter . . . horn . . . dip-switch . . . fuel-gauge . . . oil pressure gauge . . . water temperature gauge . . . lights . . . headlamp high beam light . . . direction indicator . . . flasher . . . screen washer . . . okay?"

"At just under two thousand quid I thought you might have thrown in the number-plates."

"What's that funny knocking noise?"

"Shall we drop in on the Joneses for a coffee?"

"Oh my God! . . . rain!"

"Mickey wants to know if it's got a dual choke
down-draught carburettor."

Just a little something,
compliments of
LORD MANCROFT

Season of Good Business

Christmas is upon us once again with peace in a few corners of the Earth, and goodwill (with a little bit of luck) to one or two of us.

I think, however, that when it actually comes down to details, the Chairman of Amalgamated Mousetraps may get more than his fair share of goodwill. There's a magnum of Hine brandy from the firm's Advertising Agents, two turkeys from the car-hire people, and Lord knows what else from the Company's various suppliers. This sort of thing has been going on for a long time, and I don't believe it does all that much harm, though some rather strait-laced firms frown upon all Christmas presents. They regard them as bribes for orders to come rather than as gratitude for favours already shown.

The reason I myself dislike bribery is quite simple. I'm jealous. As far as I know I've never been offered a bribe of any sort, and I take a poor view of this. It suggests two things, both unwelcome. Either I've never been considered important enough to be worth bribing, or I have actually been bribed without having the wit to recognise the fact.

Oh, now, wait a minute. I've forgotten the case (literally) of Colonel van Riebeck's oranges. The Colonel was ADC to an odd bird named Erasmus who was at the time South African Minister of Defence. I myself was representing our Ministry of Defence at a wearisome and difficult conference, the chief purpose of which was to convince Mr. Erasmus that the Russians weren't really going to drop an atom bomb on Pretoria; or at any rate not right away. Whenever the discussions looked like getting out of hand Colonel van Riebeck used to open his brief-case, and hand round oranges which apparently he grew on his own farm in the Cape. The oranges were excellent, and I naturally said so. Next Christmas a case of them arrived in my office. My secretary threw up his hands in horror. "You can't possibly accept them," he said, "they'll be regarded as a bribe, and that could well ruin all our lovely negotiations. You must send them back at once." So be it, but how? Just you try sending oranges *back* to the Cape. Fruit transportation from the Cape to Whitehall is easy enough, but not vice versa. It's like trying to get toothpaste back into the tube. Three forms

106

and four telephone calls later I threw in the towel, and offered the oranges to some children playing in St. James's Park. This gesture was not a success. Passers-by obviously regarded me as a potentially dangerous sex-maniac. The children just giggled, and ran away.

I don't know whether Whitehall is still as strict about Christmas presents as it was, but I'm told the embargo on Christmas parties in Government offices has now been slightly relaxed. These frolics used to be frowned upon not because they offered scope for bribery but because of the risk of corruption of good manners and protocol if, say, a junior copy-typist after tee many Martonis were to cosy up to the Permanent Secooretary. This practice, however, can pay dividends in commercial life, and a particularly choice form of bribery can be invoked. More than one sales rep. has earned his promotion with the help of a pretty wife's judicious attention to her husband's boss at the office Christmas party. My friends at Amalgamated Mousetraps, however, had a near-scandal on their hands last Christmas as a result of this form of bribery being carried a bit too far. At the height of the revels a certain Miss Frippett, an ambitious girl from the Post Room, staggered out of the Packing Store with her coiffure in disarray and her clothing dishevelled. "I've been assaulted," she announced, to the horror of all the company. Her friends crowded round, helped her to array her coiffure and shevell her clothing, and demanded to know who could have perpetrated such a dastardly outrage. "It must have been one of the Directors," replied Miss F. "Who else would have worn an Old Etonian tie and made me do all the work?"

"Put the Western on, son—your dad's been stuck inside all day."

Christmas also brings in its wake the problem of the office Christmas box. This is neither a bribe nor actually corruption. It should probably be regarded as protection money. If you do not acknowledge suitably the dustman at Christmastide he'll accidentally spill all the gubbins out of your dustbin, and over your doorstep on next collecting day—which is not nice if the office happens to be full of customers. It's difficult, however, to know where to draw the line, whom to box and who not. Not policemen, I hope, because it's worrying enough to read how many senior members of the CID are presently engaged in investigating charges of corruption against other members of the CID. Postmen, yes. But what about the Parking Meter people? Are they boxable, or not?

I myself would have thought they were. So, indeed, did my friend, Charlie Cringleford, who's been having a monumental row with a neighbouring firm about a parking space they both covet. But it seems that we were both wrongly advised. A few days ago Charlie sent his Parking Meter gentleman a nice bottle of whisky, and this, though apparently improper, did the trick. The Parking Meter gentleman muttered angrily about who did they think they were trying to bribe; but Charlie got the space. He told me later, however, that he had taken the elementary precaution of sending the whisky not in his own but in his neighbour's name.

There are, I realise, grey areas in the world of corruption, about which information is hard to come by. When, for instance, can you ask for your money back, and when not? Nevertheless, I still like to think that the businessman who relies for his success upon the giving or taking of bribes

"We want him to have all the things we never had."

"I can foresee the day, Yvette, when you'll be wearing the trousers."

will have a harder task in this country than in any other. I hope, for instance, that the odious J. J. in the *Sunday Express* cartoon is in real life seldom met with in the City.

I must, however, confess to being an idealist because I also like to think that the funds of our political parties are more openly come by, our commercial secrets better guarded, our offices less buggable, our Tax Inspectors less gullible, our hotel managers more ethical, our commercial journalists more perceptive, than those of any other country, and in particular than those of the Common Market which we are about to join. Time alone will tell if this optimism is justified, and if it is I'll tell you one of the reasons why.

A few days after Christmas comes the prettiest present of all, the New Year's Honours List. Now your Borough Surveyor isn't going to be caught in cahoots with a local contractor if that would imperil his OBE. Mr. T. Y. Coon will resist the temptation to indulge in hunkle-schmunkle with his balance sheet, and will continue his lavish support for the School of Chiropody at St. Egbert's Hospital because his wife would dearly love to become Lady Coon. The same goes for that pliant back-bencher whose desire to join the Knights of the Shires is recognisable in the Whips Office. Bribes, or just sweeteners? Difficult to say, but an Honours List is no hindrance to honesty.

But whatever is involved behind the scenes, a Christmas bribe should at least carry a semblance of gaiety and good cheer. Such epithets could hardly have applied to the little bag of gold offered by Lord Francis Gilmour to the executioner as he went to the block for treason on Christmas morning 1523. He begged the man to do his work quickly and well. Fair enough, for not even a traitor should be launched into the Hereafter with some oaf thwacking away at his head like a poor golfer stuck in a bunker. In this case, at any rate, you're hardly in a position to ask for your money back if things don't go quite as you wish.

"My people! The hated dictatorship is over! From now on, you will elect me democratically!"

109

"My wife says can you do something about me."

Room With a Phew

**Does London *really* have the worst hotels in Europe?
Nonsense! cries JOHN WELLS, it's all in the eye of the beholder**

Step through the memory-heavy portals of an English Inn. At once the air is densely impregnated with history. Time holds its breath, and so should you.

No one will pester or bother you. For long centuries life has gone on easily here, staining the ceilings to a mellow umber, ageing the linen with yellow reminiscence, undisturbed and stirring itself for no man. Strut, little fellow, it seems to whisper, strut and rant and bang your fist, ring, ring your jangling bell, for I have seen your like before!

Cod-pieced Elizabethans in soft beards and scented hose, come to rap with jewelled rings and lisp their petulant requests for Mr. W. S., dull, clanking Roundheads moaning about the noise at night when they were trying to pray, or verminous wits in periwigs under Queen Anne, spitting their punned spitefulness at clumsy butlers. The English Inn has seen them all, pounding the floor in rage or setting the breakfast table on a roar: has seen them laid beneath the earth, and heard the peace return.

And always peace has vanquished.

That is why you will find no ugly hum and rumble of the lift at night, or in the day time either: the stairs are quieter. No rattling trolleys bringing noisy cutlery and dishes to your room: a toothglass offers sustenance in silence. No buzzers, telephones or bells disturb your sleep, and when you wake you wake up naturally, in your own time, unhurried by alarm calls. Sleep until noon if you will, and dress on the pavement outside: the English Inn is concerned only that the room be empty for the incoming guest, an allegory of Time.

Enjoy the peace. It reigns throughout an English Inn.

In the dining room, where big Victorian flies buzz drowsily at the windows, or wander, slender-legged among the sauce bottles: where ancient waiters lean, during the brief flurry of activity from seven forty-five to eight, when breakfast's served, against the ancient furniture. The hushed rustle of

110

newspapers, the rhythmic crunching of dry toast, the infinitely slow ingestion of strong tea, and all the rest is silence.

In the kitchen, too. How different from a noisy Italian cooking range! No crackle of fat or hiss of grilling steaks, only the softest bubble and breathy pop of simmering cabbage, the plume of steam from some old blackened kettle, the chuckle of underpants boiling in a saucepan.

In the bathroom there is peace as well, and time. Time as the water trickles in, and coughs, and stops, and dribbles, and then starts again, to read the notices in blurred blue pen, that has run and dried in cloudy flowers on the puckered paper, to muse perchance on death. And shall we leave this Place as we would like to find it? Where are they now, the pale vulnerable bodies that once rested in the water in this auburn-stained enamel, leaving no more behind them than an old grey tide-mark or a rough-cut toenail? There is a brooding presence here, and history, for those with eyes to read.

In the Office also there is peace. The old-world staff who manage an English Inn are hewn from English oak, tough and sturdy and full of quiet strength. Heads bent, eyelids heavy, they wait like slumbering knights in a faery cavern, one distant day to be aroused by a magic trumpet call or the touch of an enchanted kiss. Walk among them, feel the soft hollows of their heads, test with a finger the ancient fluttering sockets of the eyes. They may stir in their sleep, as a man does who is troubled by a fly, but no mortal hand can break the spell that binds them.

And where, the traveller may ask, does all this peace and quiet contentment originate? It originates in the deep-carpeted, glass-walled offices of the American-owned Horst Wessel International, the biggest hotel group in the country. And who could not be at peace and easy in that nerve-centre of a living tradition, where men with softly gleaming heads and heavy cuff-links sit amid the aroma of cigars and count the fresh pound notes? Who could not be content and thoroughly well pleased to know that however high the standards of the foreign tourist, however luxurious his tastes, he will always be obliged, for sheer lack of competition, to spend his money at an English Inn.

To coin a very English turn of phrase, effortless success!

*"The trouble is that Ted only reminds me of Winston
when he's speaking French."*

Many of our most classic situations and expressions centre on the pleasure of drink.

Gimme a Pigfoot and a Bucket of Beer!

*American artist ARNOLD ROTH
looks at his countrymen
through bourbon-coloured glasses*

For many of us drinking is strictly a solitary
pleasure.

Beside giving pleasure, drinking encourages
religion and improves health.

We are drinking more wines lately, however, with a traditional
preference for vin du pays.

One of our greatest pleasures in drinking is the ease with which it
furthers the arts.

"It's no use. They never heard of a prince!"

Fancy
a Bit of the
Udder?

In which HUMPHREY LYTTELTON sits in the corner eating his Christmas pie

Well, well, it's nearly upon us again, eh? All right, there's no need to look like that. You know you'll enjoy it madly when the time comes. I will agree with you about one thing, though—looking forward to Christmas isn't what it used to be.

It's all too predictable nowadays. The children know what they're going to get because they've been pointing at it on the telly thrice nightly for the past month. (Until I put forward the theory that Santa hasn't got TV, I never knew that so much scorn and condescension could be invested in the three syllables "Corss he has!") We parents know what we're going to get because we're so bogged down in the preparations every year that we have to swap lists to ensure that we get anything at all. And when it comes to food, we all know what we're going to get because it wouldn't be Christmas if we didn't.

And that brings me, rather sooner than I expected, to the crux of this article. I hereby give notice that I shall not be joining you in the traditional Yuletide fare this year. Stuff your turkeys, ignite your puddings, mince your pies, tote that barge, lift that bale—Lyttelton has other plans. To cut out the shilly-shallying and come straight to the point, I shall be eating sparrows promiscuously with Hermione Waterfield.

I did think of ending the article right there, hammering out the last full-stop with an eyebrow-waggling Groucho Marx leer. But what with quarterly bills, income tax assessments and the like, enough bad news plops through the letter-box at this season of goodwill without adding a stiff and formal-looking envelope from Miss Waterfield's solicitors. So I will elaborate. Hermione Waterfield knows a lot about antiques and appears often, looking beautiful, on the TV programme *Going for a Song*. The same, with optional deletions, goes for Arthur Negus. We were all three invited by the BBC in Bristol to eat, and be filmed eating, a Georgian Christmas dinner in Georgian surroundings. The meal was prepared, with great attention to authenticity, by

114

Mary Berry, the cookery editor of *Ideal Home*, who joined us at the table. The BBC's man in Bristol, Hugh Scully, acted as host and commentator, and it was he who explained that in 1800 the fashion for deploying ladies and gentlemen alternately round the table, instead of segregated at either end, had just come in and was known as "promiscuous seating". You can see us, ranged promiscuously before your astonished gaze, on December 23rd in *Collectors' World*, so I won't go into detail about what was said and done. But the experience does enable me to hark back to the days of our forefathers and point to aspects of the ancestral Christmas blow-out which jaded turkey-eaters might care to revive.

Surveying the menu of a hundred and seventy-odd years ago, I am prompted to ask, in the plaintive, nasal tones of Bob Dylan, "Where have all the stomachs gone?". The answer, my friend, is blowin' in the wind, and you're talking to someone who knows. Our television meal had to be a truncated version due to shortage of time, and for "starters", in that ante-chamber of the menu where the demure avocado vinaigrette or grapefruit cocktail are found today, we just ate turtle soup, baked sprats, a boar's head glazed, decorated and stuffed with pâté, potted eels, a turkey glazed and dressed, chicken curry, a dish of roast pigeons, sparrows and starlings, roast duck with cucumber sauce and Neats' Tongue and Udder Pie. A neat is defined in the dictionary as any animal of the ox variety—providing, if you'll pardon an inoffensive pun at this juncture, a neat get-out for the squeamish carnivore who draws the line at plundering the intimate extremities of a domestic cow. He can always persuade himself that he is sinking his teeth into something comfortably remote, like a gnu or a bison.

Let's pause here, heaving slightly, to discuss the possibilities inherent in these opening snacks. Another interesting fact unearthed by Hugh Scully is that, in an age renowned for elegance and refinement, guests at a banquet would think nothing of plunging their noses right into a proffered dish to sniff it suspiciously before help-

"It's the gardener's day off."

"Well, well, fingers McNutty, impersonating an officer again."

ing themselves. This was good sense rather than bad manners—with poor transport and no kind of refrigeration, many of the basic materials reached the table in an advanced state of putrefaction. (Passing thought: they used spices and sauces to disguise the taste of the meat, we use them to disguise the tastelessness of the meat. Was there ever a time in between when the meat actually tasted nice?) I have to report that the huge dish of baked sprats at our end of the table grew steadily more historically authentic under the television lights as the day progressed, until we had to ask, in strangulated voices, for them to be removed. The boar's head tasted quite nice but looked horrific, mainly because someone, either in search of realism or as a sick joke, had furnished it with a pair of glass Teddy Bear's eyes. Eels, turkey, chicken and duck held no surprises, other than that they were all on the table at the same time. Leaving out of account my role as a council member of the Royal Society for the Protection of Birds, I cannot recommend sparrows. For one thing, the little fellow who hops about on your back doorstep is nearly all feathers. His unclad frame hardly furnishes more than a mouthful, and a jolly spikey, tasteless mouthful at that. Starlings are bigger and more tasty, but do we *need* them? As for udder, you might imagine, seeing it *in situ*, so to speak, that it tastes like foam rubber seasoned with a rendered-down PVC raincoat. You would be absolutely right. So, leaving udders where they belong, we pass on to the main meal.

It may be that time was pressing at this stage in the proceedings, but after the sumptuousness of the starters, the entrées seemed a trifle stingy. For one thing, we started with a disastrous soup called plum porridge, which tasted as though someone had accidentally dropped an Oxo cube into a fruit salad. From then on, it was just routine stuff—roast leg of lamb stuffed with oysters, fried smelts, a whole salmon twisted into an S-shape and pickled, a complete suckling pig so little disturbed by the cooking process that it appeared to be sleeping peacefully, a roast rabbit with its skull still revoltingly attached, a huge mince-pie actually filled with minced steak as well as the usual ingredients and, as an afterthought, Yorkshire Christmas Pie. This was rather a jolly idea—birds of various sizes boned, inserted into each other in diminishing order like those multiple Russian dolls and then baked in pastry. A large family with blunted susceptibilities might start with an ostrich and work down through the entire bird kingdom to the bee humming bird. They, and we, would be well advised to go no further, lest we find ourselves in the realms of pink pancakes tinted with beetroot, which our forefathers relished but which struck me on sight as the nearest thing to an emetic short of swallowing string.

So there it is. I hope you've gleaned some useful ideas from this little chat. I know I have. For one thing, I'm going to go straight to bed this minute with a glass of water and a dry biscuit.

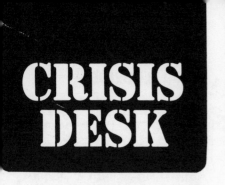

CRISIS DESK

We're here to panic on your behalf. Write and tell us your worries about the power cuts and we'll do our level best to frighten everybody sick

Dear Crisis Desk:

Last night we had to drink our cocoa in the dark. Also it was only lukewarm after over an hour with my husband's lighter and a whole box of Vestas. Is this injurious to health?

Mrs. B., Alsager.

CRISIS DESK called in nutrition analysts, a team of pessimists from Cadbury-Schweppes, the FBI and the High Commissioner of Ifni to look into your query, Mrs. B. The chief danger seems to lie in abandoning your nightcap altogether. If more than 38.2% of the nation's cocoa-drinkers were to pack in the struggle, a glut in world supplies could lead within a fortnight to an economic recession on the Gold Coast and parts of Cameroon, with an almost inevitable series of coups d'état with widespread killing, pillage and rape. There is every reason to suppose that this might quickly spread to the North. Cold cocoa can have quite a pleasant tang once you get used to it (it is highly addictive) but teeth must be thoroughly brushed afterwards as many dentists' drills are working at half-speed owing to voltage reductions and people can die from excruciating pain.

Dear Crisis Desk:

We've been stuck in a lift since Wednesday afternoon. What do you advise?

Mr. and Mrs. A., 22nd floor.

A tricky one, this, because you don't mention on your card if either of you is an orphaned pensioner with shrapnel wounds whose only source of power in your dingy tenement block is a presentation torch you got after 40 years spent down the mines. If you could write to us again (put a threepenny on this time!) and let us know also if you are cranking an iron lung machine with your one good hand, there's every chance we can get a social columnist round to you.

Dear Crisis Desk:

I am worried about the effect of power cuts on wildlife. Me and my husband live in the countryside and we love animals very much. We have a cat. Also I make jam in the summer months, so I suppose you could call us conservationists! Still, joking apart, we always try to help out wildlife from extinction during a cold snap and most evenings I leave out little knitted balaclavas in the shrubbery for the owls and mice and things to keep cosy in. And we generally leave a saucer of warmed and sweetened milk on the back-step last thing, for the hedgehog. Only last night we were blacked out and we had to leave some cold milk there. Do you know, it hasn't been touched all night!

Mrs. K., Newton-le-Willows.

We know how you must feel, Mrs. K., but it's good to see that you can still raise a smile. CRISIS DESK took up your problem pronto with an eminent vet, Whipsnade Zoo, The World Health Organisation and Bernard Braden. Experts all agree that leaving the street-lights on all day during the crisis may have permanently damaged the sensitive biological clocks inside every creature which govern their knowledge of night and day. In other words, hedgehogs everywhere may have lost all track of time! All you can hope to do is to leave your saucer out at lunchtime and if, oh if, your friend comes along, whip him indoors and keep him in a box. Place a torch over the box and switch it off last thing at night and on again when you get up. One day, if he survives, there's a chance that you can breed and keep the species sane. Take care taking in other night creatures. Certain types of voles and stoats have a nip that can maim, whilst others have voracious appetites that can get through all your furniture in a single afternoon. Switch off everything and keep your fingers crossed, Mrs. K.!

Dear Crisis Desk:

My wife works in a filament plant and is worried by reports of jobs in peril. Also, when the glow goes out, she takes almost three hours to adjust to the murky conditions and she's no sooner got the hang of things when Click! and she's dazzled again. She's covered in bruises after bumping into things and my friend says this causes tumours in mice. What do you think?

Mr. T., Oldham.

CRISIS DESK thinks you should act without delay, Mr. T.! Move all the furniture to the side of the room and surround any fixtures with cotton wool and sand. Send all your mice overseas for a little while. Then keep calm: the minute the lights go out—stop, look, listen. Try to breathe evenly and deeply and avoid sudden movements which could put a strain on your heart. Don't let yourself nibble nervously at things like candles or torch batteries as they contain very few useful vitamins and shortage of these items will quickly plunge the nation into famine, pestilence and death. If you follow these simple rules, there's a 50-50 chance that you'll both last at least until the week-end. Write to us again before then, sooner if there's any sign of fever.

Dear Crisis Desk:

Is it possible that power cuts could increase the likelihood of sudden surprise attack from any enemy power?

Mr. W., Brixham.

Certainly, Mr. W.! A week on Tuesday seems a popular guess, but looking on the bright side, there is a definite chance that we shall all be on our knees before then and that a total industrial shutdown will obviate the need for a nuclear strike and they'll move in selling beads instead. Either way, at least we shan't see them coming, eh Mr. W.?

Dear Crisis Desk:

My friend says the strike could last for at least another week. Is he right?

Miss D., Earl's Court.

Right? My God, of course he's right! This strike could last for a month, for a year, till the end of our days! Get him to marry you now while there's still time! This is a situation of appalling seriousness, don't you see! It's more serious and awful than ever anything has been ever before! And it's going to get worse! Another week of this and we're all doomed! This is the end! You must try to hang on! Switch everything off and pray! Aaaaaaaaaargh!!!

Swan Upping on the Thames.

Well dressing at Breedon Candover.

It's an Old English Custom

THELWELL'S modern folklore

The famous Horn Dance at Abbotts Dawdling.

The distribution of the Tichburn Dole.

The Battle of the Flowers — Hampshire.

Closing the Gate ceremony at White Hart Lane.

Traditional Bottle Kicking and Hare Pie Scramble, Little Hackington.

Five hundred year old Harvest Home charity at Sambourn Peverel.

"A bit theatrical perhaps, but it's quite dramatic when he bursts through."

In Praise of Crime

By HENRY CECIL

There is so much to be said in praise of crime that I find myself, like the bank-robber arrested by a Chief Constable, with an embarrassment of riches. Where would most of us be without crime? If there were no crime there would be no books or plays about crime. Look at the consternation among writers (and readers) of thrillers when Parliament abolished the death penalty. Half the suspense was gone. Some writers are reduced to saying "this took place in the days of the death penalty," but the public will not accept that for long. The joy of the thriller is that it really could happen. There are a few people who are satisfied with ghost stories or other fantasies. But most of us want to read about something which would be possible in real life. The successful thriller is the credible thriller. If no one robbed trains or banks, if wives no longer poisoned their husbands and husbands no longer drowned their wives in the bath, a substantial portion of modern literature would disappear. The abolition of the death penalty was indeed a serious blow for authors but it was not a deadly one. Messrs. Kray and Mr. Richardson (to refer to them as *The Times* would) showed that there is still enough going on in the criminal world to provide writers with ample material for an indefinite period.

Writers of fiction are deeply indebted to criminals. But where would writers of fact (and this includes some journalists) be without them? And how should we manage without the comforting headline BIG SNATCH IN PICCADILLY, which tells us at once that no war is imminent, no king has been dethroned, that butter has not doubled in price, and that there has been no devaluation of the pound and no increase of taxes or other disaster?

But this is only sounding the first introductory notes of the paean of praise. What about those whose lives are dedicated to crime and the criminals? If there were no crime it is true that

120

the police would still have motorists to play with. But what about prison officers? They would be reduced to locking each other up in cells and then letting each other out again, if only to keep in practice. And the legal profession? Where would that be? It is an established fact that the increase in crime coupled with legal aid, has not only restored the falling fortunes of the Bar but has actually made it a profession which penniless students are anxious to join. No longer has the newly-called barrister the years of bread and water and waiting, when he can only console himself by telling his girl-friend stories of cases which he has seen *other* people conduct. How long did the newly-called barrister have to wait in the bad old days before the briefs started to arrive in sufficient numbers to enable him to pay for board and lodging? Three years, five years, ten? Today it is a mere six months before he is licensed to lose anyone's case for him and to make any number of speeches in mitigation on behalf of one or more of those public-spirited individuals who live by breaking the law. Or he can even suggest to the jury that

they are actually not guilty. What should my client want to steal a bicycle for? He already has two. (Where did he get those?)

The judges could manage without crime. They would still be paid their salaries and could spend most of their time in court by tossing up imaginary coins to see who is to win in road accident cases. But what about the probation officers, the voluntary social workers and the earnest young people who want a Radical Alternative to Prison? It must give a good probation officer a considerable thrill when partly as the result of his help and advice he sees a man with many previous convictions doing a steady job, living with one wife and keeping out of trouble. But what thrill will it be when they all keep out of trouble? And what will the earnest young people do when there are no prisons to want Radical Alternatives to?

And think of the officials in the Home office spurring on successive Home Secretaries to try and get more and more money out of the Treasury to build bigger and better prisons. For many of them it would be the end of the road.

"Are you sure it's me you love—or just my tunnel?"

Let Nothing You Dismay

GRAHAM has the family in to drink to that

"*And for heaven's sake, this year try to exude a little bonhomie.*"

"*How about a big kiss for your Uncle Arthur?*"

No new prisons, no new borstals! It's unthinkable.

And what about prison chaplains and prison visitors? Even Members of Parliament (who periodically shed tears when someone refers to the degrading practice of slopping out, still maintained in many prisons) would have to find some other evil to deplore and ignore.

And what about private security organisations? No more money to be escorted to banks, no more bejewelled old ladies to be protected, no more vans to be robbed in lay-bys.

And when you think of the amount of employment which crime gives to honest members of the public and the amount of entertainment which would be denied to us if there were no crime, it is a sombre thought that the people who get the least out of it are the criminals themselves. There are, of course, a few who make crime pay. They constitute a very small minority, but let us be thankful to them too. For they help to keep the whole movement alive. Without them some of the most interesting episodes in criminal history would never have occurred. They themselves make the best of both worlds. With no previous convictions they are eligible for election to many respectable bodies, they can even be parliamentary candidates and who knows if every now and then one of them may not slip into the legal profession? Fortunately he can never rise to the top of that profession. No highwayman has ever managed to get on to the Bench. It's as well for criminals that this has never happened, for sentences by criminals on criminals would be astronomical. To teach them an important lesson—not to be of good behaviour but not to be caught.

We need not worry about the future. Fortunately successive British Governments have realised for the reasons which I have mentioned and no doubt for others too that it is necessary in the interests of the nation that crime should go on. How otherwise can one explain their failure to take my advice and double the police force?

122

"Now take this Rhodesian situation."

"She's not **my** aunt! . . . I thought she was **your** aunt!"

"Once the Queen's broadcast's out of the way, we'll get the hell out of it."

"Must you go?"

"I wondered if we should have volunteered to help with the washing-up."

The Glass that Cheers

The drunk joke which hiccoughed across so many pages of the Victorian *Punch* was grim recognition-humour. The intoxicated were an obtrusive part of most people's environment. Because the paper hated poverty, it hated the conditions which caused the flight to alcohol; but in those unideological days it was quite possible to hate the sin and laugh at the sinner.

Drunks were grotesque imitations of humanity, like babies or monkeys or the Irish. Whether the tipsy were arguing outside a jug-and-bottle, showing confusion during an after-dinner speech or returning late to a Mayfair home to be met by a hostile wife at the head of a grand staircase,

they provided fun which was both affectionate and contemptuous. Only recently did this hard-worn joke fall victim to the developing sensibility which had already banished jokes about religion, infirmity and race.

Where you got drink, you got reformers. *Punch's* attitude resembled Dickens's—objects good, methods bad. It justifiably slammed the teetotal extremist. (Keene's temperance orator loudly orders soda and whispers the instruction to put a glass of brandy into it.) The movement to shut down pubs got no support, though there was, apparently, something to be said for locking up the drunkard rather than his tipple because that could do good as well as harm. Better the

DELICATE TEST

Elevated Party. "*A never think a fl'er's had t'mush wine s'long as a windsup-ish wash!*"

[Proceeds to perform that operation with corkscrew.]

1859

DEFIANT DEFINITION

Barmaid. "*We never serve Anybody who's had Sufficient; you've taken too much already—*"
Thirsty Customer. "*You'll 'xshcushe me, Maram! I may've 'ad too mush* (hic), *bu' I 'aven't 'ad Enough!!*"

1872

"*Are you comin' 'ome!*"
"*I'll do ellythik you like in reasol,
M'ria—(hic)—Bur I won't come 'ome.*"

1895

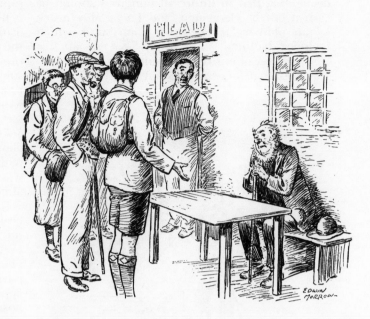

OUR PROGRESSIVE COUNTRYSIDE

Visitor. "*Oh, just four pints of bitter, please, and perhaps the old gentleman here would like to join us.*"
Oldest Inhabitant. "*Thank you, kindly, Sir, I think I'll have a short one. Just a dry martini and a spot of absinthe.*"

1930

pub, anyway, than the unregulated pastrycook's where wine and spirits were genteelly sipped by ladies.

However, when the publicans unctuously supported the bishops in opposing Sunday excursions, *Punch* saw through them. Its stance was ambivalent; but, on the whole, it sympathised with Keene's drunk who asked plaintively why he should be deprived of "neshary refreshment" because another party didn't know when he had had enough. Ever grateful for a simple jest, it was much amused because one member of a deputation to the Home Secretary on Dipsomania was a Dr. Lush.

Punch was suspicious of legislation, however benevolent, and reported with delight that the teetotaller Sir Wilfred Lawson had told a worried House of Commons that it might need an Act of Indemnity for keeping an unlicensed inn. Nothing was done about it; but many years later A. P. Herbert initiated an unsuccessful prosecution for selling liquor illegally.

The social standing of urban inns seems to have declined after the days of Dickensian euphoria. In early *Punch* they look cosy, fuggy and spartan: you sat on hard wood and the floor was sanded or sawdusted. Gradually the London bar, scene of so many characterful conversations between beery tipplers or spiritous harridans, faded out and it was the rural delights of the village inn that got the half-pages. This change of focus was part of the urban nostalgia for a countrified past which was so strong in the paper before and even after World War I. It was permissible for a city gent to drink his English ale in a centuries old hostelry by the village green, especially if it had low beams, gleaming brass and yokels wise and foolish.

Looking back through the volumes, with every intention of keeping to the point (drink), I couldn't help noticing a couple of irrelevant oddments which deserve to be shared. There is an amused note about a petition from Rochdale pointing out in horror that the demeanour of

125

executioners was often insufficiently grave, and demanding that in future all hangings should be carried out by clergymen, and I was also struck by an obituary tribute to a contributor which included the lines,

Maker of mirth and wholesome jokes;
Fit mate of dear ROSINA VOKES.

*"Can you recommend a
medium dry champagne
suitable for launching a ship
of twenty thousand tons?"*

1939

Change was slow in the drinking world, or nonexistent: as Raven-Hill's toper remarked, the pint pot didn't hold any more despite all the progress hymned at the Jubilee. The great days of bibulous experiment belonged to the period between the Wars, though Phil May drew one innovator who had invented a new drink—whisky and soda, but more whisky. Women returned from the services flaunting their emancipation by wearing short hair and skirts, dancing at tea and drinking cocktails. What these were was left in decent obscurity. (There is circumstantial evidence that in 1924 the Editor, Sir Owen Seaman, had never heard of pink gin.)

Across the Atlantic came rumours, at first incredible, of Prohibition. This fascinated the paper and horrified A. P. Herbert, who actually went over and looked at it close to. *Punch* was wholeheartedly against it for a number of reasons, not all convivial. Typical was George Morrow's New York traitor asking a client

whether he wanted his hip-pocket pint or half-pint size.

By the time of World War II, inability to find drink had replaced inability to stand up to it as a theme. Black market spirits became a currency, a proof of out-smarting rival drinkers and the subject of beautiful daydreams. With quantity unavailable, attention switched to quality, and wine snobbery was no longer confined to a small sector of the aristocracy and learned professions. Jokes about obtrusive oenophiles replaced jokes about clinging to lamp-posts or coming home with the milk. The trouble is that the real thing was so preposterous that burlesquing it was almost unnecessary.

In the past quarter-of-a-century, drinking has been treated mainly from the point of view of hospitality: there are many pictures of parties in overcrowded rooms with the drinks carried round on trays and conversations either at cross-purposes or pessimistic. Hewison showed appalling insight into the relation between a host's looks and his attitude to refreshment. One moustached householder is labelled, "Oh dear! This means you are going to get a 'Ferguson Special' (if Ferguson is the man's name), poured liberally and repeatedly from ready-mixed jugs. The dangerous alcoholic qualities of this drink are laughingly denied by your host before anyone has thought of suggesting them. It consists almost entirely of orange squash."

Philip Oakes reported some strange detail about "Pop People's Drink." In Glasgow they like Treble Up—half of bitter, a tot of red wine and a small scotch, mixed in the mouth and swallowed in a gulp. Six years before, a pub on the Dover Road had sold practically nothing but brown and mild; but the spread of continental holidays made customers clamour for vermouth and lager with lime. Sales of lager rise in Lent.

"Boy! What a party!"

1952

E. S. Turner conducted an enquiry not into drinks but into what went under them. Southern England required only half the beer-mats found necessary by populations further north. There is a British Beer Mat Collectors Society (Presidents: Morecambe and Wise). An American mat carries a message in invisible ink which emerges only when beer is slopped on it. Collectors of mats are called tegestologists.

One big change over the period is the restraint of the temperance lobby. These days pornography and marijuana have diverted the publicity-prone from the fight against liquor. Non-drinking can be for non-teetotal reasons. David Langdon's husband standing at the bar asks his wife, "What are you off for political reasons *this* week? Port and lemon, Algerian wine, Russian vodka . . ."

There have been signs that the supporters of soft drugs are hitting back by attacking tobacco and alcohol as drugs of addiction. Perhaps one day they will launch a full-scale campaign on Victorian lines, Band of Hope and all. And what a godsend to *Punch* that would be.

1950

"*How many doses did you give Daddy?*"

1961

127

Do-It-Yourself Tax Form

*Mr. Barber's idea for a simple tax form is all very well—what we need is a tax form you can **really** do yourself. Here's how.*

Is this the first time I have ever done
my own tax form ?

Yes

Will I declare that everything in this form
is correct to my best knowledge ?

Yes

I do know, don't I, that a false return is
liable to severe penalties ?

Get on with it !

Sorry. Where was I ?

Making out my tax form.

Of course. What is my name ?

George Nisbet

Where do I live ?

23, The Lane, Ruislip

How much did I earn this year ?

£ 2,300.

Am I married ?

Oh, for heaven's sake!

Yes, I know, but I can't just put down " I
am married ", can I ? It's got to be all
question and answer, hasn't it ? Eh ?

Sorry

Well, then. Am I married ?

Yes.

How much did I earn this year ?

I've asked me that already.

Oh, yes. Well, that's about it, then, isn't it ? *What about expenses, etc ?*

I'm ∎ quite right. What expenses do I claim
against income from my business? Good Lord -
I quite forgot! What **is** my business ?

I am a plumber. I claim a small van against tax.

What about advertising ?

NISBET! The Reliable Plumber!

No, I mean do you claim advertising expenses ?

NO.

Well, that's it, then. *Then how do you explain your shares, your country house, your Rolls and so on ?*

Ah. Yes. Well. Look, I may have given the
impression I'm a plumber. It would be truer
to say that I'm a sort of tycoon, but I can
explain everything. Can we go on to another
sheet ?

It had better be good.

Boom, What Makes My House Go Boom?

By ALAN COREN

"One of the effects of the house-price spiral and the rush to buy has been that estate agents no longer find it necessary to disguise the truth about their properties."—*The Observer*

I met him at the gate, as arranged. We looked up at the house together. He glanced at his watch, not unobviously.

"It's rather nice," I said. "I've always wanted to live in St. John's Wood."

"No point going in, then," said the agent, taking a cigarette from his packet and deftly avoiding my reaching hand. "This is Kilburn."

"Oh, surely not! I understand that this area was traditionally described as, well, as St. John's Wood borders?"

He sucked his teeth. He shook his head.

"Not even Swiss Cottage," he said. "Not even *West* Swiss Cottage."

"Swiss Cottage borders?" I begged.

"Kilburn." He put the watch to his ear. "If that."

"Oh."

"What do you expect," he muttered, "for twenty-three-nine-fifty?"

"Twenty-two-five," I corrected. I showed him the specification sheet.

He tapped it with a finger.

"Got yesterday's date on," he said.

"I received it this morning," I said, "and surely——"

"Lucky we put a threepenny on," he said. "Might be out of your range tomorrow."

"Could we go in?" I enquired. "It's rather chilly here."

"What do you think it is inside?" he said. "Bermuda?"

"The central heating must make a——"

"*Part* central heating," he said. "Plus small boiler, totally inadequate to

"You realise, of course, that this will cost you both a merit star?"

129

"Glad to see you're with us."

the job. Especially bearing in mind the lack of double-glazing. The only way to tell if the radiators are on is to put your cheek up against them and wait for a minute or two. Still, at twenty-four-two-fifty, you can't really complain, can you?"

"I suppose not," I said, "these town houses are at a premium, these days."

"*Terraced* houses."

"I always thought——"

"Call a spade a spade, that's our motto. When you've got a long line of nondescript jerry-built bogus-regency items leaning on one another to keep from falling down, they're known as terraced houses. Or, in some cases, back-to-backs. If the gardens are as tiny as this one is." He opened the front door. "Don't rush in," he said, "or you'll miss it, ha-ha-ha!"

"Ha-ha-ha!"

"See that crack in the hall ceiling? You'd think they'd take a bit more care with a twenty-six-grand property wouldn't you?"

"It doesn't look too bad," I said, "probably just a fault in the plastering. A good workman could fill that in in two shakes of——"

"That's what the previous owner thought," said the agent, stubbing his cigarette out on the wallpaper. "His dog fell through it and broke its neck. Treacherous, these stone floors."

"But sound," I said. "No chance of warp, dry rot, that sort of——"

"You wait till your plumbing packs up," he said. "Main conduit's under there: one day your bath's cold, the next you've got six blokes and a pneumatic drill poking about in your foundations. Want to see the kitchenette?"

"Thank you."

"'Course," he said over his shoulder as he forced the door, "when I say foundations, that's only my little joke. Three inches of builders' rubbish and a couple of two-by-fours, and that's it. I wouldn't like to be here when the motorway goes through—one articulated truck, and you're liable to find yourself with half the roof in the downstairs lav."

"Oh, I didn't realise there was a downstairs lavatory," I said. "That's rather encourag——"

"I wouldn't show it to you," he said, "I wouldn't even talk about it. Not so soon after breakfast. This is the kitchenette."

"We've always encouraged Polly to join in the conversation . . ."

"Damn 'New Statesman' reader, I shouldn't wonder."

"Kitchen*ette*?" I said. "Mind you, I suppose it is a bit on the small side, but——"

"*Small?* It's lucky there's no mice here, otherwise you'd have to take turns going to the larder."

"Well, you wouldn't expect mice in a modern house, would you?"

"Right. Rats yes, mice no."

"Oh. Well, we've got a cat, so——"

"That's one bedroom out for a start, then," he said. "Big cat, is it?"

"Neutered tom," I said.

The agent pursed his lips.

"Probably have to give him the master suite, in that case," he said. "At least he can shove open the bathroom door and stick his tail in if he starts feeling claustrophobic. Lucky it's on the first floor, really."

"I'm sorry?"

"If the cat's on the first floor, you and the family can sleep above it. On the second. You don't want a bloody great moggy stamping around overhead all night, do you? Let alone watching you and the missus through the gaps in the floorboards. Lying on your back listening to the tubes rumbling underneath, with a bloody great green eye staring down at you."

We left the kitchen, and came back into the hall. He opened another door.

"I imagine that's the dining-room?" I said.

"That's what you want to do, squire," he said. "Imagine. Mind you, it'd do for buffet suppers, provided the four of you all had small plates. The other door leads to the integral garage, by the way, if you were wondering what the smell of petrol was. You've got a car, I take it?"

"Yes."

"Don't forget to leave it outside, then. Bloke two doors down made the mistake of changing his Fiat 500 in for a Mini. Brought it home from the

131

"I think it's terrible, putting a man of his age on motorway patrol."

showroom, drove straight in, had to spend the night there. Wife fed him through the quarterlight. I suppose you could always have a sunshine-roof fitted, though."

"We'll leave ours out," I said. "It's more convenient, what with taking the kids to school every morn——"

"Oh, you won't need the motor for that, squire! School's only a stone's throw away."

"Really? Well, that's a load off——"

"Very good glazier up the road, though. Mind you, you have to take the day off to let him in. He won't come out at night."

"That's surprising."

"In this neighbourhood? After dark even the police cars cruise in pairs."

"Do you think we might go upstairs?"

"And that's only if there's a full moon."

"Four bedrooms, I think you said?"

"Well, three really. The third one's been split into two with a party wall, but you could easily convert it back. Just slam the front door, and bob's your uncle."

I started up the staircase, and it wasn't until I'd reached the first landing that I realised I was alone. The agent called up.

"You all right?"

"Yes," I shouted.

He joined me.

"Hope you don't mind," he said. "Never tell with these stairs. I reckoned you were about my weight." He patted the banister lovingly. "See that workmanship? They don't make 'em like that any more!"

"It's certainly an attrac——"

"Not after *Rex* v. *Newsomes Natty Fittings Ltd.*, they don't. Christ!" he exclaimed, looking at his watch again, "it's never twelve o'clock already!"

"Two minutes past, actually."

"That's another half-hour off the lease, then." He turned, and started down the stairs again, gingerly. "I trust you have the requisite used notes in the motor, squire?"

I followed him down.

"I'd like a little time to think about it," I said, "and then, of course, my solicitor will have to make the necessary searches and——"

He laid a kindly claw on my arm.

"Do yourself a favour, son," he said gently. "Forget about searches. Tatty old drum like this, you can never tell what they might find. Now, look, am I going to be able to unload this or not?"

"Well, I'm not entirely certain, but——"

"I suppose my success is due to a mixture of luck and good judgement: I collect the market forecasts of a dozen or more chartists and fundamental analysis experts and then pick one of them with a pin."

"He chose the wallpaper himself."

The agent wrenched open the front door. A queue stretched down the path, and into the street. Mute supplication blinked in their watery eyes.

"Says he's not certain!" cried the agent.

Instantly, the queue dismembered itself into a shrieking mob.

"One at a time!" yelled the agent, tearing a brassette carriage-lamp from the wall and beating a clearing among the grabbing throng. "Let's do this proper! Now, I am not asking twenty-nine-five for this mouldering pile! I am not asking thirty-one-two-fifty, I am not even asking thirty-two-and-a-half, all I'm asking is——"

I edged through the pitiful clamour, and out into the road, and bent my steps towards the YMCA. It's warm there, and there's a nice peg for your anorak and a shelf for your clock, and it'll be weeks before the developers start bidding for the site.

With luck.

The Health Food Fad

by
HEATH

"*Better make it half a pound—I don't think I could carry a whole pound.*"

"*I don't eat it man—I smoke it.*"

"*Oh him, he's one of my regulars.*"

"*Ah—the groaning board.*"

SUMMERTIME AND THE LIVING IS EASY?

HARRY SECOMBE
unpacks his summer stock

Summer shows come in three different sizes—the small, seedy, end-of-the-pier show, the medium-sized, elegant, top hat and tails variety, and the big, brash, family-sized star vehicle, expensively costumed, spectacularly staged and occasionally disastrously box-officed.

In the first kind, the principal comedian is probably someone who has seen better days and can be found most afternoons in the nearest local to the pier, recounting his past experiences. So you'll know where to look for me in a few years' time. There is often a husband and wife who sing duets and act like cooing doves on stage. Off it, however, they become birds of a different feather. Mr. Novello's lilacs which they have just gathered so harmoniously turn to hellebore the moment they get into the wings.

"Can't you sing in bleedin' tune?"

"You can talk, you were so off key even the pianist noticed it."

Then they will go back on stage and bow sweetly to non-existent applause.

To complete the company, there will undoubtedly be a conjuror who doubles as compere and spends too much of his spare time stuffing silk handkerchiefs into cardboard cylinders and retrieving white doves from the roof of the theatre to pay much attention to the soubrette, who will be in her mid-thirties and constantly talk about her one television appearance in 1958. And that was on the Nine O'Clock News.

The chorus girls will be called Betty, Muriel, Shirley or Doris. The pianist will be a lady but will look like a man, or vice versa.

135

"It was a damn silly place to put the cafeteria."

The second type of show is more genteel and a higher class of entertainment. The company plays Pavilions rather than Piers and travels its own wardrobe mistress, stage manager, musical director, but not, unfortunately, its own audience.

The content of the troupe will be similar to the first show, but there will be more of them. The principal comedian will be reasonably well-known—in concentric circles—and will have a stooge who will also act as dresser and drink his booze when his back is turned. The comedian's wife will not be in the show, but will sit out front to make sure that nobody else gets the laughs when her husband is on. This will cause trouble with the second comic early on in the season, and the company will then divide itself into two factions—those who are loyal and want to work with the star next season, and those who are disloyal and don't care whether they ever work with him again. The latter group will get smaller as the show reaches the end of its run, and will finish up consisting of the second comic.

The ladies of the chorus will be called Daphne, Fiona, Hermione or Susan-Jane. The musical director will wear a wig.

The star vehicle is brassy and big and designed for the largest theatres in the seaside resorts. It will have rehearsed for two weeks in London and will be produced by a West End impresario. If it has a female singing star, the dressing room will have been completely redecorated, at her insistence, before she moves in, and when she does arrive she will complain about the smell of paint and develop a sore throat.

The costumes and scenery will be brand new, and the show is bound to have a grand spectacular scene where thousands of gallons of water are pumped twenty feet into the air. At the final dress rehearsal something will go wrong, and thousands of gallons of water will be pumped twenty feet into the stalls. The impresario will leave for London by ambulance.

The whole of the second half of the show will be taken up by the star, and it is a safe bet that before the end of the first week the microphone will have been changed at least twice; the first four rows of the stalls will be deafened by the amplification of the star's supporting group; and there will be protests (a) that she cannot be heard at the back of the theatre and (b) that she can *still* be heard at the back of the theatre.

The dancers, or show girls, will be called Midge, Jackie or Frankie, with a suspected Fred. The musical director will wear tight trousers.

It may seem that I am exaggerating, but I have experienced all three types of summer season and the audiences that go with them. There was the time when I was told by a flat-capped gentleman, as I left the stage door of a Blackpool theatre, "You nearly had me laughing when you were on." It was a compliment.

That is precisely the attitude to first nights I used to come up against when I was a second spot comedian. It was my job for years to go on after the opening and break down the resistance of the audience for eight minutes while the stage was prepared for the next scene.

I remember standing transfixed in the centre of the stage on a South Coast pier, like a small Welsh zeppelin trapped in a web of enemy search-lights.

"Hello there, folks. Welcome to the show. Are you all enjoying yourselves then?"

"Yes!" shouted the bass player who was drunk.

No one in the audience bothered to answer, because it consisted in the main of landladies with free seats, given to them in the hope that if they liked the show they would tell their boarders to come to see it. They sat unsmiling with arms folded and ears akimbo for the expected innuendo.

I have attempted to raise smiles from an audience which has had to battle its way in a force ten gale along the pier to get to the theatre. By the time they were seated, the steam began to rise from their wet clothes, and I came out to face what appeared to be a low flying swamp.

"I see we've got a good cloud in tonight," I quipped. They sat in soggy silence.

Audiences vary tremendously in summer resorts, especially towards the end of the week. Normally a show gets its best and biggest houses on a Saturday. Not so at the seaside. Saturday is change-over day, when the old holiday-makers go and the new visitors arrive. Whey-faced and uncertain of their new surroundings they are more interested in settling down than going to the theatre. It is then, after the euphoria of a great Friday night second house reception, that the blaze of indifference of a first house Saturday re-awakens in the depths of one's soul the suspicion that there are more worthwhile things to do than trying to dredge laughs from reluctant throats; that there is more to life than a belted aria.

Then comes Monday and a wonderful first house, and the journey back to the digs through the smell of fish and chips and candy floss, and the sound of raucous singing and breaking bottles of Tetley best bitter is a joyous one, because if they were like this tonight they're going to be sensational tomorrow night. And of course they never are . . . but just wait until Wednesday.

"Hi Mac—whichaway Shangri-la?"

137

It's Love that Makes the Rain Come Down

By ANN LESLIE

What men or gods are these?" cried Keats to his Grecian urn: "What maidens loth? What mad pursuit? What struggles to escape?"

What struggles to escape, indeed. The maidens are obviously far from loth, and aren't escaping at all, merely beating a temporary tactical retreat.

After all, if they're not there for a spot of jolly rustic rape, what *are* they there for—skipping winsomely about like that in the undergrowth, draped in bits of ill-fitting scarf, bared bosoms bouncing about like beanbags? Clearly such saucy misses were always hanging about in Arcady waiting for some godling to ride by, or even a herd of corpulent satyrs to come thundering out through the olive grove with twigs in their hair and bunches of grapes dangling about their privates.

No, the maidens' anxious glances obviously are not directed at their pursuing lovers, but at the terrain: any minute now, if they don't pick up speed, they'll be flung down in some nettle-patch or bit of dank bog and used as a sex-object-cum-lilo—and too bad they didn't quite make it to that cosy patch of ant-free moss ahead where they'd planned to sink prettily to earth in strategic surrender.

It's about time really that the liberated nymphs of the seventies turned rapist in order to avenge women's centuries of ordeal by alfresco sex. Womanhood must now wheel around and leap off in hot pursuit of yelping lovers as they scamper desperately over cow-pat and thistle, felling them with neat karaté chops and seeing how much *they* fancy being ravished in a gorse bush for a change.

Of course, you could reach some kind of compromise by suggesting the use of a groundsheet—although such a measure tends to be viewed with lofty contempt as being yet another, typically feminine attempt to destroy the essential spontaneity of outdoor eroticism. Moreover, it's a direct attack on his virility: how dare you *even* suggest that being impaled on a bramble bush could materially diminish your ecstasy once he's treated you to the full splendours of his sexual technique?

Back home in Barons Court, your feller may well have been mugging up on the secrets of the 143 positions received under plain brown cover, but let

138

him come within sniffing distance of meadow or copse and you can forget all about that: as far as Man is concerned, Woman's sexual position in the great bug-filled, horsefly-haunted outdoors is always, quite literally, inferior. A chap feels so much safer that way . . .

I once had a boyfriend whose principal erotic ambition was to make love naked in the snow. I was to peel down like a grape glacée, but he'd be all togged up as usual, snug as a bug in his Lillywhites' oiled socks, ski-boots, string vest, fair-isle woollies, long coms, y-fronts, stretch pants, furry mitts, anorak, pompon hat and goggles.

Okay, I said sourly I'd do it, but only if he took off his clothes as well. He found the suggestion profoundly lewd: *"Me?* Take off my *clothes!* Who do you think I *am?* And besides," he added in pained reproof: "You *know* I get chilblains."

I retorted rudely that *my* joints would play up something horrid once he'd deepfrozen me into the Eigergletscher, and how about *that* lover-boy? and he retorted sulkily that I wasn't very romantic was I, no imagination, in fact downright *frigid* he'd say. And I yapped back that I certainly *would* be frigid if I went in for many such Sex-on-Ice Spectaculars, and he said very funny, ha, ha, and eventually went off, masculine modesty still intact, and found himself a massive Finn who simply adored roguishly romping about in snowdrifts while being beaten on her big pink botty with a birch-twig . . .

If snow is nasty, beaches are nastier. There's nothing less passion-provoking than lying prone in the freezing spume, with seaweed making rubbery squawks and pops beneath you and little sudsy waves playfully filling your eardrums with gritty foam and rendering you deaf as a post for hours. You emerge rubbed raw, beaten flat and encrusted with sand like some jumbo-sized wienerschnitzel ready bread-crumbed for the pan.

In fact sand is highly inimical to enjoyable sex. One girlfriend of mine,

"One day, my boy, all this will be yours . . . how about tomorrow?"

having reached the age of twenty-five, got bored hanging around Saving Herself for Mr. Right, and decided to go on holiday to pick herself the sexiest Mr. Wrong she could find.

She lit upon a Spanish squid fisherman called Miguel—who surged about in the gigolo's regulation crotch-strangling jeans, raking every female under ninety with his fierce, steaming glances—and decided she'd have to surrender her All to him on the beach, since that's where he seemed to spend his life when he wasn't actually out at sea, or under it, or surging profitably in and out of wealthy widows' bedrooms.

The experience was horrendous and she swears she's been right off sand, and virtually off sex, ever since.

Boats aren't much better than beaches. Small boats have skittish ways and tend to tip you both into the harbour oil-slicks, more often than not in full view of shrieking boat-loads of unspeakable schoolboys with braces on their teeth. Large boats are generally better—although it does rather depend how many devotees of love-making under the stars are crammed on to any one boat at any one time.

I was once on a working cruise round the Adriatic islands with a bunch of randy travel-agents of both sexes who, swiftly awash with slivovic and freed from the pruderies of home life in Crouch End and Potter's Bar, paired off—and then spent the whole of the first night reluctantly playing Sardines en masse on deck.

All night long, the yacht rang with muted thumps and twangs and clonks as frustrated lovers softly ricocheted off steel ropes and anchor chains and fire-buckets, desperately hunting for a patch of unoccupied deck, occasionally uttering stifled grunts and hisses like "Ouch!" and "Oops!" and *"Muriel!"* and "Sorry old chap!" and "What the hell . . .?" and "****!"

From below one could dimly hear them blundering about like a herd of blinded elk, and none of us on board got a wink of sleep that night, and judging by the uniformly filthy tempers of the star-crossed adulterers next morning, they'd not been able to get a wink of anything else either . . .

Incidentally, have you noticed how people still wax absurdly lyrical on the subject of outdoor sex in our rural past? One can still stumble across sentimental parlour-Rousseaus who'll bore you rigid with explanations

Four Red Stars *ALBERT'S Soviet Hotel*

"*If you require anything, sir, just speak into the table lamp.*"

" '*Growth and development of heavy industry in the Caucasus' is on at the ABC Minsk.*"

about how all those lads and lasses having it off in haystacks were, in some primeval way, acting out folk memories of fertility rites among the ancient corn gods.

Actually I think they were always having it off in haystacks because it was more convenient than having it off at home—what with the place being full of cattle and pigs and hens having fits and the wimminfolk a-guttin' rabbits and the menfolk a-packin' dung and Grandma stickin' pins in wax dolls and some spavined cousin a-layin' of the hired girl behind the butter churn as usual.

Spirituality scarcely reared its pretentious head one suspects, in truly bucolic sex: you got yourself a good woman if she had all her own teeth, proved to be good breeding stock by dropping a lusty son every nine months—and then stoutly shaking her skirts and going straight back to work again, bashing beets and strangling chickens.

Idealisations of rustic lust were still being produced until relatively recently, largely by middle-aged literateurs whose slim volumes on rural Venuses tended to be financed by Papa's liver-pill fortune or great-aunt's Brazilian holdings, and whose knowledge of nature was pretty well limited to what they saw out of train windows on day trips to Box Hill.

Oddly enough one *can* be made to feel dimly guilty about not liking sex out there under the skies, in the great embracing bosom of nature.

For after all, is one not Woman—whose great groundswell of spirit apparently answers to the ebb and flow of the seasons, whose blood is said to rise with the sap, wild calling to wild in the core of her being, whose soul they say lies deep-rooted among the burgeoning mysteries of bogmyrtle and bladderwort? Whose breasts are like the hills, whose eyes like stars, whose hair like tangled moonbeams; who's as capricious as the summer's day, and yet full of deep intuitive wisdom; the fleshly expression of the universal life-force from whose fecund loins springs the eternal Manchild . . . and all the rest of the Earth Mother codswallop.

And do you mean to tell me that this mighty mysterious spirit isn't keen on a bit of slap and tickle among the bog iris *merely* on account of it's cold and it's wet and the sea fog's rising?

Yes, I do.

"*It says additional bathroom facilities will be incorporated in the next five-year plan.*"

"*Tipping is bourgeois, and offering will offend the workers'dignity, so we include it in the bill.*"

For the pageant that opened the old
London Bridge in Arizona they had to
train the Indians to paddle canoes.
HONEYSETT wonders what other
skills they may have lost

*"Mr. Rockobeat has kindly
consented to come along to
demonstrate a blood
curdling scream."*

"Just don't blame me when you get cold at nights, that's all!"

"Look, will you tell your wife's late brother to clear off so that we can get through to the rain gods."

"Perhaps we're supposed to use more than one ant."

"It's no good, we just can't get near them."

"Another two here for scalping."

Coming Out in the Open

MICHAEL PALIN

WATCHING television does not come easily to the complete novice, but with perseverence and application the enthusiast is rewarded with one of the most attractive and worthwhile outdoor activities known to man. That man is: Mr. Edward Birds of 14b, U Thant Buildings, Huddersfield. It was in the Spring of 1968 (or '69 as it was later to become) that Ted, as he is known to the trade, first introduced me to the techniques of television-watching as an outdoors sport. The contestants sit, or "slump" as they call it, in front of a cathode ray tube, or "cathode ray tube". The tube is then turned on, and the contestants are bombarded with streams of electrons made up into random and apparently pointless images. The first to lose his mind completely is known as "The Controller of Programmes" and has to retire.

There is little that can stir the heart of an Englishman more than the sight of that cool expanse of greensward, the buzz of the occasional bee, the linnet in the hazel tree, the click of the switch on the set, and the soft blue glow of the cathode ray tubes on the faces of the contestants as they vie with each other to test their strength of mind against the massive onslaught of meaningless electronic particles.

But, you will say, isn't it dangerous? Why do these fit young men—the flower of their country's youth—and not only fit young men, also decrepid old men and even moderately unfit middle-aged men, and also women of no particular physical condition whatsoever . . . why, you will repeat, why do they risk their health and mental stability watching television out of doors, when they could be killing small animals or falling off mountains? Ah . . . in the words of that famous old Himalayan television watcher: I have to watch it . . . because it's there.

JOHN WELLS

SPARROW coursing! There can be few experiences more apt to fill the cistern of the soul with effervescent happiness than that of bursting through a thorny brake on a summer morning, with the crystal drops a-scattering from the leaves and the dogs a-snuffling at one's heels, to surprise a fully-grown male sparrow ruffling its under-feathers on a well-sprung twig. Then a shrug of wings, a blurred, whirring swoop under cover and the hunt is on, hounds with their tails up swinging their velvet nostrils left and right in search of Brer Sparrow's scent among the grass, the red-faced huntsmen toiling up the hill, or pausing to press a strident silver horn blast echoing up the valley to signal "Sparrow Away ZZZ!" What memories of Chaucer's "uppe atte sparwefarte", what thrill of figuring in tradition's tapestry, what sense of pageantry beneath an English summer heaven as Mister Sparrow weaves and ducks and doubles back, hanging immobile upside down from boughs to feign a wasp's nest, hopping along a distant twig to mock its followers, conceding at the last after a damn good day of exercise that he's enjoyed as much as any huntsman, to have his liver tossed among the dogs, his feathers dipped in gore to blood the novices! And finally, with bright glass eyes, a head upon a wooden shield in some great trophy room, to stir an old man's memories of one day, long ago, among the fields and fells of Merrie England.

"*He doesn't say much but he's a very good listener.*"

BERNARD BRADEN

MY favourite outdoor activity has always been tennis. Not so much for its advantages as a game as for the psychological delight of taking part in a competitive world to the point where it doesn't much matter whether you win or lose.

But I didn't fully realise the attraction of this side of tennis until I took part in a doubles match with Stephen Potter who, I'm glad to report, was my partner. He elected to serve first, to a young undergraduate who was as keen as mustard and kept bending his knees and swaying from side to side as if he was about to receive Rod Laver's fastest serve. He kept on bending and swaying as Potter went through an elaborate series of rituals prior to serving. At long last Potter raised his racket and hit the softest, highest serve ever to cross a net cord. The undergraduate rushed forward hastily and slammed it feverishly way out of court.

As Potter and I crossed over for the second service, he leant over to me.

"Aced him," he said.

"*Why don't you come and live in our tax haven? . . . What's it called again, Emily?*"

GEORGE MELLY

FLY fishing—especially for sea trout at dusk on a Welsh river—an activity so uncertain that the occasional fish in the net carries an almost unbearable atavistic triumph.

Fishing gives me an illusion temporarily of being a very old man with pale slightly mad blue eyes, beyond sexual anxiety and with no one left in the world who might want to telephone me. To walk towards the water through clouds of midges—golden specks in the rays of the setting sun—provides the least ulcer-provoking moments of my life.

Emptying a wader full of water and pulling it on again over a wet sock and sodden trouser leg is not only exquisitely uncomfortable but makes me feel manly.

Not losing a fly which has become caught in a tree makes me feel both lucky and clever. Zooming through the Welsh night on a motor scooter at 15 m.p.h. is about as much excitement as I, a cautious creature, can bear with.

Getting cold enough to justify a treble brandy in my local pub is much less guilt-making than simple alcoholism. Re-entering the cottage and pseudo-casually throwing a smallish sea trout down on the slate slab gives me more satisfaction than finishing a book.

TERRY JONES

OF all outdoor activities known to man, possibly the healthiest, most exciting, and at the same time most socially beneficial is that of "lynching." The limbs are wonderfully exercised in running about and generally holding down a struggling victim, in climbing trees, pulling on ropes and that sort of thing. While the lungs are given great ventilation in the practice of shouting obscenities and screaming with hatred. Certainly nothing can compare with the excitement of a really top-flight "lynch mob" first setting eyes on its victim: the air is filled with sound, the blood rushes to the head, and the everyday cares of family life are forgotten in a spontaneous feeling of comradeship and a fulfilling sense of purpose. And then again, a single "lynch mob" can accomplish in a few moments what an entire population has been wishing to do for years.

It is all the more of a tragedy, then, that there exist so few facilities for lynching in this country today. Try as they might, even some of our best-loved politicians have been able to do little more than create a climate of opinion in which the "lynching party" may yet become an acceptable part of our everyday life.

In the meantime, enthusiasts like myself must content ourselves with reading the Daily Telegraph, and dreaming of the day when our favourite outdoor activity shall once again be lifted out of the living room, away from the television sets, and brought out into the open . . . on to the streets where it so truly belongs.

FRANK MUIR

'A garden is a lovesome thing, God wot.'
God! *What?*

My own ill-favoured thing is lovesome for about nine minutes per annum. This brief rapture, when the assorted boskage has reached maturity and the garden is a riot of colour, mainly green (grass) and brown (earth), occurs from roughly a quarter to three to roughly five to three on the afternoon of the eighteenth of July. The only year when I was not away on holiday during those few precious moments somebody rang me up and I missed them anyway. During the rest of the year the garden is in either a state of labour-consuming, conscious-pricking growth, or is sinking into ugly decay.

Man's puny attempt to subdue his corner of the jungle is pathetic, really. Any gain is only temporary. Mow the lawn. Pause but a moment to dampen the back teeth with a little beer and the grass has sprouted an acne of daisies. Miss a week with the clippers and the hedge does its Ken Dodd impression. Victory over nature is not possible. This spring I mastered the daisies with a powerful—and I hope painful—poison, and bought an electric hedge-trimmer. Result? The weeping-willow died. Just dropped everything and stood there, unbelievably naked, like an unfrocked umbrella. And the electric hedge-clipper committed suicide by severing its own umbilical cord.

I have now come to a conclusion. My favourite outdoor occupation, garden-wise, is devising the quickest honourable way of nipping back indoors.

JOHN CLEESE

MY favourite outdoor activity is tarring and feathering myself. My father taught me how to do this. He lived in Bombay between 1921 and 1923 and he used to tar and feather himself as a way of attracting attention at Garden parties. People at the Bombay Yacht Club had normally ignored him as he was an uninteresting conversationalist and also because he had learnt "Pilgrims Progress" by heart and would always manage to work the conversation round to Bunyan and then start quoting. Anyway, all you have to do is to coat yourself with tar and then take a bus somewhere where there are lots of loosely supervised chickens. Then just pick up a few as though you were examining them for an official reason and surreptitiously wrap them firmly against your tacky hearts. You should soon be feathered enough for ordinary purposes. Now the world is your oyster.

"I was hoping to break into films."

"And do these folk know you're singing about them?"

What Shall We Tell the Parents?

A child guerilla's Christmas Plan,
vouchsafed to KEITH WATERHOUSE

Xmas Day minus 12, countdown begins. My Father keep asking me what I want Xmas. You cannot just have Parcels in this house, you have to make out a List. It go up the chimney, after he have crossed out Bicycle and also copied it out, he thinks I don't know but I do know, I have seen him. The list is supposed to go to Santa Claus. There is No Such Person.

Xmas Day minus 11. I have made out my List. I want a troch, bicycle, fort, Whizzer & Chips Annual, pen that lights up, That Game, as well as Box of Smarties, American jail-wagon, also Parcels. I would rather just have Parcels. In this house, the Things that you get, for Christmas, they are just put on the bottom of the bed so that, you can see them all at once, when you wake up. A person should not able to see them all at once. They should be Parcels.

Xmas Day minus 10. (What on Earth is a blessed Troch?) vouchsafed my Father, at the same time reading my List.

146

"My programme is to increase harvests, cure the economy and get some statues made."

(It is like a pen that, it lights up, but, it does not write) I ejaculated.

(Oh, a "Torch") groaned my Father. (I have a good mind to ask Santa Claus to bring you a Blessed Dictionary.)

(And another thing, what on Earth That Game when it is at home?) continued that worthy. (Is it Monopoly, Ludo, Snakes & Ladder, or what?)

(It is called, Mousetrap) I vouchsafed.

You should not begin a sentence with the word, And.

Also, you should not vouchsafe that, Santa Claus no room on his Sleigh for a bicycle, when, what you mean is, certain persons are too mean to buy one.

Xmas Day minus 9. Today my Father caught me looking in Linen Cupboard. (What doing in there, lad?) he ejaculated, but, he did not say anything. This mean that, he has not bought my Presents, yet.

Xmas Day minus 8. Today my Father caught me looking in Spare Room. (If you do not stop prying and poking in, places that do not concern you) stormed The Latter, (I shall tell Santa Claus not bring you any Presents). This mean that, he is going to Get them tomorrow.

If he could really talk to Santa Claus, you would not have to put List up chimney. Why should you have to post List up chimney, if, you can talk to him. Elementary my dear Watson. There is No Such Person. It is Your Father.

Xmas Day minus 7. (By the way, lad) exclaimed my Father, (I do not think that Santa Claus can find you a Mousetrap Game).

This means that, he has Got Them.

Pouring himself a whisky, my Father continued his narrative. (And Santa Claus wants to know, what Earth is a blessed American jail-wagon?)

(It is where the Sheriff puts them in, when they have been caught. The bullion robbers) I maintained, adding for good measure, (You can get them at Hamley's.)

(I am not going to blessed Hamley's again!) he

147

vouchsafed quickly. He given himself away. It is Him all the time.

Xmas Day minus 6. My Xmas presents are in My Father's Wardrobe. I have found them. I have got, 1 torch, 1 fort, Box Smarties, 12 Soldiers, 1 pen that does not light up, Rotten Dominoes, also Pencil Box, also 1 Rotten Book. I have not got, 1 bicycle, 1 pen that lights up, 1 Whizzer & Chips Annual, 1 Mousetrap Game, 1 American jail-wagon. The Rotten Book is entitled, (The Children Encyclopedia). This is not a real Present, it is like School. Another example is, the Pencil Box. They should not say they are Presents, they should just give you them. In this house they do not just give you them, they crack on they are Presents.

There are no Parcels, they are just in paper bags from (Hamleys). This proves that there is No Such Place as Santa Claus's Workshop, Reindeerland, North Pole, The World, The Universe, Space, Outer Space, The Galaxy.

Xmas Day minus 5. Today My Father go Purple. (What been doing in my Wardrobe?) volunteered he, adding for good measure, (You prying little Monkey).

(I have not been in Your Wardrobe) vouchsafed I, but all in vain. (Then why is there a Chair in front of it?) ejaculated my Host, adding for good

"Friends . . ."

measure, (You not deserve Christmas Presents, I am going to give them all away to the Poor Children).

He knows I have seen them, therefore, he will have to get me Some More, or, it will not be a surprise.

Xmas Day minus 4. He has taken them out of the Wardrobe. Also, they are not in linen cupboard, boot-hole or pantry. The tool-shed is another example. I will find them.

Xmas Day minus 3. Today, I asked my Father how Santa Claus, can take all the Presents round, when there are so many children, in the world. (Ah!) gasped My Father. (Most of the Presents are delivered by the Fairy Postman, and then Santa Claus drops the Rest of Them down the chimney on Xmas Eve).

This means, that, he has got Some More. He has got an American jail-wagon.

Xmas Day minus 2. They are in the Cistern Cupboard. I have not looked at them, as, it would not be a surprise. I have just felt them, with my eyes closed. I think I have Broken the American jail-wagon.

Xmas Eve, blast-off. Tonight, I could not sleep. My Father kept looking round The Door. He looked round The Door at ten o'clock, half-past ten, eleven o'clock, twenty-past eleven, 10 to twelve, five past twelve, 25 past twelve, also one o'clock. He go all Purple and start shouting, (If you not asleep in ten minute, I am going to ask Santa Claus not to come). I heard him opening Cistern Cupboard door where he has Got Them. Also, I heard him vouchsafe to my Mother, (Next year he gets a sleeping tablet before he goes to bed). He is going to Drug me.

Besides the Other Things, I have got, 1 Mousetrap Game, 1 Whizzer & Chips Annual, 1 Set of Matchbox cars (got them already, if He did but know), also 1 Dective Set. I will use this for Finding Things Out.

Xmas Day. Today I woke My Father at Five O'Clock by the means of, shining my new torch in his eyes. (Look what Santa Claus has brought me) I volunteered. He Swore. This means, that he will go to Hell.

Later, he came down for Breakfast. He would not mend my American jail-wagon, or play Mousetrap. He is the same as Scrooge. (You go to all this trouble, and he not play with Things for five minutes) ejaculated My Father, adding for good measure, (We will know better next year). He say this, every year.

Why I like Christmas is, you can watch telly at, breakfast-time. You can watch (Tom and Jerry), also, (Santa Claus) but, it is not him, it is just somebody Dressed Up.

148

GENTLEMEN
FARMERS

MAHOOD

"Why is it, if you want anything done properly you've got to do it yourself?"

"Shouldn't your cows know you by now?"

*"And at what time does **he** deign to get up?"*

"Just think, we've been doing it wrong all this time."

HORSE OPERA

By WILLIAM HARDCASTLE

I went racing over the holiday weekend.

This is rather unusual for me, though if you climb on my roof (which I'd rather you didn't) you can see Epsom grandstand.

The best way to strike up a conversation in the pubs round here is to know what won the 2.30 Selling Plate at Thirsk last Michaelmas. I am encircled by training stables, four-footed friends clop around the local lanes, and manure can be had at a very reasonable price.

In spite of all this my ignorance about the Sport of Kings is pretty profound. This originates from my acquaintance with the men who write about horse racing for the newspapers.

These come in two distinct types. One affects a curly-brimmed brown trilby hat, loud, monotone voice and binoculars on the rear-window shelf of his car.

He refers to trainers as Spiffy or Paddy, and will tell you that the Derby second favourite was sweating ominously after a mild canter in the home paddock a couple of mornings ago. Of course, he will confide, it all depends on the amount of rain we get between now and the off. In other words he always has a string of excuses for being wrong.

The other type of racing correspondent is a man of pale visage, though often with a dyspeptic nose, and suffering from extreme short sight. He goes under the nom-de-plume of Colonel Oddfellow, or some such. His indoor appearance is accounted for by fact that this is where he does all his work—inside the office.

The pebble lenses to his spectacles are necessary for the translation of the

150

fine print of the voluminous records and form books that he pores over each day. He may not see a blade of grass or a fetlock from one Ebor Handicap to the next, but, as long as he keeps his nose to his books and does not venture near a race course, he's a man worth listening to.

So, as I sharpened the nodule of my shooting-stick the other morning, I was selective in the advice I took from the morning prints. I also pondered on the wonderful generosity of the men who were making my outing possible—the race horse owners.

It is true to say, I think, that few owners do it for the money. The jockeys prosper, or the most successful of them do. The trainers manage to eke out a living. But the owner must be a well-britched man, and do it for the game (though what is sporting about yelling to a failing nag in the last furlong, or, alternatively, leading it into the winners' enclosure, is not clear to me).

But, in certain circles, the owning of a string of overbred fillies and geldings is highly regarded. I've heard it suggested that a successful man's order of priorities, status symbol-wise, is as follows: a Rolls-Royce or Bentley, a country place, a mistress, and then bloodstock.

But it is not only the *nouveaux riches* that we have to thank. There are plenty of *vieux riches* around the sport as well, and this leads one to another intriguing aspect of horse racing—its extraordinary social variety.

It is possible to bump into Lord and Lady Etonanarrow, chatting to a Royal personage or two, in the paddock, and then stroll only a few yards to come on an extremely common punter whose nerves are as evidently frayed as his cuffs. Wander among a race crowd and you will encounter some fairly squalid rinsings of humanity cheek by jowl with the sort of people who make William Hickey pull out his notebook and scribble.

The Jockey Club, the organisation which runs the sport, is composed of men of impeccable bloodline, but an equally integral part of the sport are

"Willoughby only joined for the looting and the raping."

"I hear he's too embarrassed to be seen begging . . ."

the seedy bookmakers, the tipsters, the hangers-on, the coves and the winkers, whose habits, never mind their parentage, leave much to be desired.

This fine social stratification in horse racing is also indicated by the amenities that some courses provide. You can find sanitary facilities that might have been imported from Devil's Island in the middle of the last century—all this, and more, within a stone's throw of a representative selection from Debrett's and Burke's Peerage eating strawberries and cream and emitting tinkles of laughter.

But no such sordid thoughts were passing through my mind the other day as the horses went up the course for the start of the first race. I had been given an excellent, if none too solid, lunch, and my hopes ran high, even though the binoculars were proving difficult to focus.

I was also heavily engaged in that mental arithmetic with which race-going is inextricably mixed. Four-to-one, I can understand. But 100-to-6 is much more difficult. Especially for someone who always has difficulty in remembering the difference between "on" and "against".

I nod wisely but stay silent when people nearby start talking about doubles and cross-doubles and trebles and Yankees. These are quite beyond me. A similar sense of inadequacy occurs when I go to the paddock. To *me* all the horses look good. Again a dumb nod is all I can offer when the excessive length of a beast's back, a faulty haunch, is pointed out.

In any case additional information is what I definitely do not want. The racing editions of the evening papers will tell me ten times more than I want to know about any one horse, its parents, its age, its weight, its past performances, and its preferences in the matter of the ground under hoof. Multiply this by the number of horses in the race, add the huge and conflicting variety of tips that are so readily volunteered, and you will understand that when I go under starters' orders I am usually in a state of high confusion.

This is why my sparse race-going career is dotted with disasters. Backing the wrong horse, throwing away the wrong tote tickets, and so on. Remember, too, that I am incapable of understanding a race once it is under way, and you will have correctly grasped that I am not the most perceptive of race-goers.

Well, can *you* see what's going on? It is given to people like Peter O'Sullivan and John Rickman to discern the fly on a jockey's riding crop at three miles, but I find the sorting out of one horse and jockey from another, at full gallop, absolutely impossible.

The situation is not helped by the race commentator who, in the hysteria of the final furlong, usually becomes unintelligible, and I have to wait for the numbers to go up on the board to find out what won. Oh, yes, that's *another* thing that's happened—I have torn up a winning tote ticket in misapprehended disgust.

Yet, all in all I had a good day the other day. Made some money, too. If this goes on I might contemplate buying a string of status symbols myself. Just think of me, in the paddock, inspecting my steed. Trouble is that I'd probably pick the wrong horse there, as well.

"Come on down, Evans—it's all been a silly mistake. Your wife forgives you and wants you to go back to her—but only if you want to—your boss also wants you to return to work and is willing to give you an extra ten pounds a week, and the Council have found you a new house and a nice flat for your mother-in-law . . ."

"Well, that's the luck of the game."

"Lies! All Lies!"

by ffolkes

"I don't think I'm ready for stardom yet."

"I didn't know it was loaded."

"I'm up to thirty a day."

"Your little secret is safe with me, Henri."

"I'm sure you'll outlive me by years and years, Donald."

Country Life

Not everything that happens in Britain gets into the national press. This feature, to which readers contribute, presents some of the news which never made it.

While rescuing a hedgehog which was being attacked by an owl at Throop on Monday night, Mr. James Cunningham, a Securicor patrol officer, was bitten on the forearm by a bat.

(Western Gazette)

Manchester City Council has decided, as a protest against apartheid, not to allow a party of South African engineers to visit the city's sewage works next year.

(Birmingham Mail)

Coun. H. Gawthorpe presided at last week's meeting. He reported that, in response to the advertisement for a caretaker for the Burial Ground, only one application had been received. This was from the person already doing the work. The meeting decided he should carry on.

(Worksop Guardian)

Mr. George Oxtoby, pictured in last week's "Express" with a giant runner bean, asks us to point out that he is not moving to a bungalow next year.

(Skyrack Express)

"He may not be the rightful King, but he looks a pretty handy lad to me."

When he was being questioned about his behaviour in King Street, Knutsford, a man pulled a dead fish out of his pocket and hit a policeman across the face with it, a court was told yesterday.

(Manchester Evening News)

The wards, which incorporate the latest devices for cleanliness and happiness of the patients, include the use of disposable compressed paper bed pans made from used football coupons.

(Glasgow Herald)

He died suddenly in 1920. Cutting his fingernails one day, the scissors slipped, wounding a finger. Blood poisoning was diagnosed as gout and he died shortly afterwards of heart failure.

(Gloucester Echo)

Walsall Library Committee has bought a cat for £190.

(Birmingham Evening Mail)

For seven hours a man defied police from a 60ft high roof. Then they brought in a woman and child to help persuade him down. She called to him: "Come down, pet, I love you." But when the man still refused she called: "Jump, then, you bloody idiot, and let's get home."

(Scottish Express)

" Yes, but on the credit side the smell's completely disappeared."

156

When Mrs. Charlotte Welford, 62, of axmundham Road, Aldeburgh, drove nto the back of another car in Aldeburgh, all she said to the other river was, "I am Benjamin Britten's ister" and drove off.

(Leiston Observer)

he magistrates heard that a "fierce truggle" ensued during which the onstable's testicles were grabbed nd squeezed . . . Fining him £30 or 0 days in prison, chairman of the justices, Mr Alfred Playle, told him e should not take the law into his wn hands.

(Braintree & Witham Times)

arwigs love to crawl into something ollow and hide in the daytime, and ome out at night. There are two chools of thought about how to take dvantage of this.

(Bury Free Press)

"*Have you noticed how empty life seems when the tortoise has gone into hibernation?*"

"*You're Common Market and Ulster, aren't you? I'll hang on for Soccer and Racing.*"

Gavin was again seen, this time in a telephone box in Victoria Avenue. Asked what he was doing, Gavin replied: "Making a phone-call." Gavin was obviously drunk and was arrested.

(Morley Observer)

Gents black overcoat, long length, worn by undertaker, now retired, good quality, but one shoulder slightly worn. Phone . . .

(Liverpool Post)

Malcolm Blog (20), warehouseman, of Catford, was fined £20 at Tower Bridge when he pleaded guilty to stealing two shirts and a panti-girdle, the property of British Rail.

(South London Press)

Otford parish councillors are anxious to borrow a small inflatable dinghy or boat to repair the duck house on the village pond.

(Sevenoaks Chronicle)

The committee is suggesting that the council should appoint a toilet cleaner and give him a bicycle to help him to get from one toilet to another quickly.

(Rhyl Journal & Advertiser)

Mary Catherine Jones, of no fixed address, admitted stealing the pork pies, value 18p, from Marks & Spencer Ltd., and recklessly damaging two angel cakes and a steak and kidney pie.

(Mansfield Chronicle)

When police were called to investi-ate a theft at her flat, 17-year-old andra Thornton offered them a cup f tea and a biscuit. But the officers ecognised the biscuits as part of a aul of confectionery stolen from rystal Palace Football Club two days arlier.

(Croydon Advertiser)

To milk a polar bear, you first lure it into a meat-baited snare. Once in the snare, which does the beast no harm, you shoot an anaesthetic dart into it. Within 10 to 15 minutes, the bear is harmless and you can milk it the way you would any other bear.

(War Cry, Organ of the Salvation Army)

Country Life continued

P.C. Gordon Wilkinson said that Catchum was wearing a maxi-coat, flowered hot pants, knee-length boots, pink glasses, make-up, and carrying a handbag. He said he had gone into the toilet for natural reasons.

(Exeter Express & Echo)

A chance remark made by funeral director Mr. David Webb at Leighton and Linslade Chamber of Trade and Commerce annual dinner may result in 100 tons of cod heads being delivered to his home.

(Beds & Bucks Observer)

Gravedigger Fred Stubbs rarely hears the telephone ring when he is at the bottom of a 9ft. grave.

(Yorkshire Post)

McNicoll said in court: "She knocked me over with the pram and then hit me on the head with a No-waiting sign. This is what happens every time I see her."

(Edinburgh Evening News)

Police say they caught Vasquez and Evaristo Guedez red-handed as Vasquez tried to stretch the neck of a dog called Champion to make it look more like a goat.

(New Zealand Herald)

"I knew we should have drawn the line at the two woodworm..."

At the end of yesterday's meeting, Councillor Eric Collins said he wished to raise a point under "Any Other Business". The matter was, he said, any other business. Councillor Edward Sakne, the chairman, ruled that any other business could not be discussed under "Any Other Business" because the council had just agreed to scrap it.

(Birmingham Mail)

Mrs. Buckingham told the court: " have worked for British Rail for te years. I am very sorry and ashamed."

(Crewe Chronicle

People who have met Mrs. Nora Spence, former Mayoress of Lincoln only on some civic occasion wher she had nothing of any consequenc to do with her hands, can only have very limited idea of what she is reall like.

(Lincolnshire Echo

Said chairman Ald. Jack Margret "But, of course, if there are an further cases of indecent exposure then we shall look at it ver carefully."

(Rochester & Chatham Pos

Dr. Wearn has a great family interes in the Pacific. His great-great-grand father, the Rev. J. Williams, wa eaten by cannibals in the Solomo Islands.

(Sydney Sun-Herald

Belfort, France: A railman entere hospital at Belfort for removal of hi haemorrhoids and got his nos straightened. Dr. Jean Butzbach tol a court who fined him £150 for hi error: "It struck me that the middle o his nose was bent."

(Southern Echo

"I wish you'd stop bringing your work home, Gerald."

The Object is Not Only Not to Win, It's Not Even to Take Part, Either

A select list of Christmas games for adults

Postman's Knock

This game is usually played throughout the Yuletide season, i.e. from about November 9 onwards. It also goes by the names of Dustman's Knock, Butcher's Knock, Newspaperboy's Knock, Grocer's Knock, and Remember-Me-I'm-The-Man-Who-Came-The-Year-Before-Last-To-Do-That-Outside-Drain-Of-Yours Knock. The rules are fairly simple: the householder waits in an upstairs room with the curtains drawn, peering through a chink; as soon as he sees one of the other contestants coming down the garden path (it is the first time since last Christmas that they have taken this route, having otherwise preferred the longer, but more picturesque, trip via the azaleas, the newly-sown grass, and the lobelia

bed), he rushes around the house switching off the lights, radios, etc. and locking such things as children and dogs in a sound-proof cupboard under the stairs. The Postman/Dustman/Andsoforth then knocks. After ten seconds, he knocks again. After a further ten seconds, he pokes open the letterbox and cries: "Merrychristmasappynewyearguvnor!" The other player has to remain absolutely silent. If he makes a noise, he pays a forfeit (anything up to a fiver). If he remains silent, however, he pays a forfeit (anything up to a dustbin on his Rover).

Hunt The Slipper

Almost every family in the land will be playing this extremely popular game over the next few days. At some time during the seasonal junketing, the doorbell rings; the householder's wife goes to the door, and cries in a penetrating voice "HALLO AUNTIE RITA!" This is the signal for the householder to leap from his drunken glaze, race up the stairs, and begin rummaging through a large pile of tartan felt objects in a corner of his bedroom. He is trying to find the pair of slippers given him by Auntie Rita. This is not easy, since he has been given at least fourteen pairs of slippers, all of which he not only hates but has also managed to detach from their accompanying cards. This is a curious game: while the odds on his finding the correct pair and so winning the prize (of having Auntie Rita come in and stay until the cheap ruby port has run out and her funny hat has come down over one eye) should, mathematically, be fourteen-to-one, they turn out in practice to be something in the nature of four-thousand-to-one. No-one has succeeded in explaining this phenomenon, least of all those men one tends to find on the fringes of funerals, weeping uncontrollably over not having been invited to attend the reading of the will.

Hyde Park Corner

All of us, of course, played this game as children, or, rather, as pubescent teenagers. The adult version, however, has rather less necking. Basically, the householder's brother-in-law turns up at the householder's Christmas party (usually with an amusing electrical device wired invisibly to his right palm which knocks the fillings out of your teeth when you shake hands with him, and a blonde in fun-fur hotpants who subsequently does a strip and/or is sick on the householder's bank-manager) and collects all the male guests in one corner of the room, leaving the women to stare at one another's clothes. The brother-in-law then tells an extremely interesting story lasting two hours about how he's just driven the Jag from Maidenhead to Hyde Park Corner in forty-one minutes and eleven-point-three seconds according to his Rolex chronometer, which was, by the way, the watch chosen by the Helsinki Olympics Committee and is guaranteed to one second per month, which is not bad for only four-hundred-and-seventy quid, is it, 'course that's the wholesale price I'm talking about. This game is over when the male guests, who happen to be the only friends the householder has in the world, start looking at their Timexes and their wives and drifting out into the night. The brother-in-law then collects his prize, which is usually about seven bottles of scotch.

160

"It must be Christmas again."

Consequences

An extremely enjoyable game, this, particularly since it need not be restricted to the householder's own family circle, but may be extended almost infinitely. Nor is there any strict ruling on procedure: the game usually starts haphazardly, and just builds up. A typical example might begin with the householder giving his son an airgun, say, for Christmas; and the householder's neighbour giving *his* son a rabbit. The gun is used to shoot the rabbit, and the rabbit is used for shoving in the householder's face, on Boxing Day afternoon. The householder then withdraws the neighbour's invitation to the householder's booze-up, and the police join the game at midnight when the booze-up is at its height in pursuance of enquiries as to complaints laid under the My Wife And I Are Trying To Get Some Sleep Act, or some such. All the players then leave to be breathalysed, and the householder goes out and kicks the neighbour's fence down, after which the neighbour throws a brick at the householder's greenhouse. The game is over when the first For Sale placard appears.

Pig In The Middle

The householder sits at one end of a long table, his wife sits at the other, and eighteen morose relatives sit between them. The householder then takes a large roast animal and begins to carve until all the meat is off the bone; he then wraps his hand in bandages, and starts to carve the turkey. This having been at last accomplished, the thirty-six eyes of the other players leave him and follow the platter of meat as the householder's wife carries it around the table, and each player in the middle forks what he considers to be a decent portion onto his plate. The platter then returns to the householder, who eats the feet.

Musical Chairs

The game begins with eight comfortable chairs in the householder's living-room, and eight players sitting on them, including the householder. At this point, an elderly aunt belonging to the householder's wife turns up with her middle-aged bachelor son, unexpectedly. The householder gets up from his chair while the other players stare at him, and goes upstairs to get a chair from the bedroom and a stool from the bathroom. The object is to bring these two down together, not singly, thereby enabling the householder to gouge a track in the staircase wallpaper with the chair, and knock two banisters out with the stool. As soon as he arrives back in the living-room, the doorbell rings again,

and he runs to open it, watched by the other players; to find his wife's cousin from Weybridge who was just passing through on his way to somewhere he *had* been invited, ha-ha-ha, and thought he'd drop in with the jolly old season's greetings. And his wife and her grandmother. The cousin and wife join the other players, leaving the householder to carry in the grandmother, who bites him under the impression something untoward is happening. When the householder gets to the living-room, all the players stare at him again. This time, he has to go up to the attic to get three folding chairs. As he is coming downstairs with these, they begin to unfold, skinning the householder's shins, and knocking off the top of the newel-post. This continues until the householder either runs out of chairs, or is taken away.

Statues

You will all have played this as children—one player has his back to the rest, and when he turns they have to freeze in position—but it's much more fun in its adult version. Basically, the householder moves among his guests, chatting, filling glasses, and so forth, and obviously not able to keep an eye on everything. From time to time, however, he turns suddenly, and everyone stops: the object is to catch brothers-in-law nicking handfuls of cigars, pocketing half-bottles of gin, touching up the householder's wife (except in the case of blood-relatives) and so forth. Anyone caught doing anything like this wins a poke in the mouth.

Simon Says

A favourite Christmas game for more competitive wives. Should the conversation turn to Red China, the devaluation of the dollar, private education, the escalating cost of Concorde, the Labour Party schism, or indeed anything else, Simon's wife (or Nigel's, or Roland's, or Henry's) interrupts with "Well, Simon says . . ." and proceeds to quote at length. Simon (or Nigel, or Roland, or Henry) takes no part in this game, he merely sits in the householder's favourite chair smiling his fatuous bloody smile and getting more and more smashed on the householder's single malt.

Ten Green Bottles

The householder's favourite Christmas game. When the party is in full swing, the householder goes out to the garden shed with a case of the best and stays there until about December 29th. There are no other players.

161

"Don't you think you ought to stop them now? It keeps spelling out rude comments on the Moroccan Burgundy."

The Games Grown-Ups Play

by QUENTIN BLAKE

"Eh, lad, why can't you be a sport and dress up like the rest of the family?"

"*We've established that he's 19th century, connected with the arts, and begins with a B; now we're trying to find out if he's a painter or a musician.*"

"*ll say it's a good hiding place; it was hristmas '69 when we invited you.*"

"*Now come along, Simon—you've got to tell us where you've put those pieces.*"

"*f course, we've been to the National Theatre once or twice recently, so it doesn't seem so bad to us.*"

Maybe It's Because I'm Not a Londoner

By GEORGE AXELROD

"Well I couldn't stand the ulcer-making rat-race pressures of Madison Avenue any longer, so I came over here, took things easy, relaxed, got myself a modest job in a small London agency. Wow—it was great. But you British (forgive me) are so godamned lazy and inefficient. In two years I had the agency reorganised. In three years I became a Director. In four, the Managing Director. Opened a branch in Paris to handle foreign accounts, developed a European organisation—Stuttgart, Amsterdam, Stockholm, Milan . . . I'm thinking of getting away from it all and settling for the simple life in Tasmania—with maybe a modest job in some small agency."

An American newly settled in London enjoys certain advantages not granted to his British neighbours. A subtle but important one is that his social mobility is not impeded by his accent. American speech of every social level falls with an equally appalling thud on the British ear. The aristocratic, "Eastern Establishment" noises emitted by, say, the late President Kennedy appear to be indistinguishable from the harsh gutturals of a Bronx cab driver. Both are lumped together under "American Accent" and from that point you're on your own.

Let me just define "Social Mobility." Not long ago we were privileged to spend an evening with Duncan Sandys. We discussed, among other things, hanging, the restoration of. "If you favour hanging," I asked, "why stop there? Why not drawing and quartering?" "Can't get the horses," he replied with the kind of deadpan British comedy that I have come to find irresistible, in a macabre sort of way. He later favoured us with several choruses of *Miss Otis Regrets.* Although I deplore his politics, I found him utterly charming.

The following night I was standing in a corner discussing revolutionary tactics with Richard Neville. Although I deplore *his* politics, I also found *him* utterly charming.

Perhaps the above examples are poor ones, demonstrating, as they do political rather than social mobility. Although, you must admit, Duncan and Richard are an unlikely combination for anyone with a British accent to meet on successive evenings. Anyhow, let me try it another way. While we were re-doing our house a workman was laying tiles on the floor near the bar. It being close to five in the afternoon, I found myself irresistibly drawn to the bar area. The workman and I chatted for a moment. Emboldened by my clearly American but not socially *placeable* accent, he felt free to inquire, in what I took to be deepest cockney, if the small, signed but undated Picasso drawing on the table were not perhaps a 1904? (It was a 1905).

In the same way, at the bar at Whites' (where I had been kindly invited to luncheon) a hearty gentleman of the (to borrow a delightful line from P. G. Wodehouse) "There's a lot of good stuff in old Reggie. And more going in every

164

minute" type, cheerfully confided that he had never read a book in his life.

The point being that, had I spoken with the accent of "Old Reggie," the workman would never have dreamed of discussing the early work of Picasso with me. And had I spoken in the accent of the workman, I doubt that "Old Reggie" would have confided the secret pride he felt in his own illiteracy.

"But why did you choose *London?*" many Londoners have asked since we settled here three and a half years ago. The man must be mad, their tone implies. With all the legendary splendours of America, Disneyland, Las Vegas, Times Square and Beverly Hills available to him, why would he come *here?*

While Americans can be lumped together by accent they cannot be lumped together by attitude. In my own case, my profession (and I have never quite been able to decide what it is; I usually put "Playwright" on the little cards they give you to fill out just before the plane lands, but only because it sounds more dignified than some of the other things I do such as writing pieces like this) permits me, within certain limits, to live wherever I choose.

I first came to London, as a guest of the United States Army, in 1944. I was young enough and dumb enough in those days to find something Hemingwayesque and romantic about air-raid sirens and falling buzz-bombs. There was a young lady of course, vaguely connected with *Time-Life.* And the splendidly bearded gentleman who, after standing me two pink gins in a pub off Piccadilly, politely asked me if I would care to flog him.

The whole thing was love at first sight.

My second visit to London was in 1953. I stayed at the Savoy as a guest (more or less) of Binkie Beaumont. The play I had brought over turned out to be a hit and ran a year at the Aldwych. Nothing gives you a warmer feeling

"Pardon me, we're from New Orleans—would you call this foggy?"

about a city than to have a hit play of yours running in it.

After that, we returned to London many times over the years, shifting our allegiance from the Savoy to the Connaught and building an ever-widening circle of British friends. So . . . on a certain ghastly moonlit night, when the Hollywood movie industry was shot out from under me while crossing the ridge and Chasen's restaurant was empty and grown men were tearfully turning in their swimming pools, we decided the time had come to get out of town. New York was, even then, impossible. The Parisians spoke French. London seemed the logical choice.

We (my wife and I) had decided, for reasons not nearly so snobbish as they sound, that we would try, as far as was decently polite, not to huddle together with the rather large and ever-growing colony of Hollywood expatriates, but to attempt to take advantage of a new environment and enrich our lives by meeting new people. *English* people, by God!

Our first *new* friends started out as our landlords. The charming young couple from whom we rented and later bought our house in Chester Square. From there we spread our antennae slowly outward. All I knew of our next door neighbours was that their name was Channon, that he was a Member of Parliament, and that they had what appeared to be a lunatic addiction to a recording of *Lily the Pink* which they played endlessly and at full volume just behind our drawing-room wall. Meanwhile, all the Channons knew of us was that we had a seventeen-year-old son who had discovered it was easier to break curfew by climbing from his attic window, across the Channons' roof to the house of a school friend whose hours were more liberal than his. En route, it had become his somewhat morbid pleasure to pause at the skylight above the Channons' nursery and make alarming faces through the glass, thus terrifying the otherwise unflappable Nanny Channon.

These unhappy events brought, most happily, Paul and Ingrid Channon into our lives. He and I met, each to complain to the other. The Channons, I discovered, had a new baby who could only be lulled to sleep by the strains of *Lily the Pink*. The phonograph was in the library, young Henry on the top floor. Hence the volume. By mutual agreement the phonograph was moved to the nursery and Steven was advised on pain of death to use the stairs when he wished to sneak out at night.

Kenneth Tynan was a good friend from the days when he was in America reviewing plays for the *New Yorker*. Through him and his beautiful

"He reads too many comics."

and brilliant wife Kathleen, we were to meet everyone of interest in British show business, from the cast of *Oh! Calcutta!*, to HRH The Countess of Snowdon. (She was fully clad on the occasion of our meeting, but otherwise, gracious and charming.)

The British Film Institute, displaying a perversity unequalled even by the *Cahiers du Cinema*, extravagantly admired a number of my more disastrous films and permitted me to deliver a John Player Lecture which was later televised, much impressing our wine merchant and greengrocer. Further television appearances followed and for a happy, Camelot-like period, I reigned as Resident-American-Authority-On-Almost-Everything, not to be displaced until the arrival of S. J. Perelman. London, I discovered, can deal with but one American humorist at a time. (Look out, Sid, I hear Art Buchwald is coming!)

You may have noticed that, thus far in this essay, I have not used the obligatory word that Americans are expected to say when asked why they have removed to London.

"Civilised."

Okay. It will be remedied forthwith.

As we were once again remodelling our abode (as some women are said to be most beautiful whilst with child, my wife is never more beautiful than when she is with house), our contractor, Bill Wynn (it would be "Sir William" if I had my way), noticed late one afternoon—it was during the time of the

166

dustmen's strike, and garbage was piled high in Chester Square—that flowers and messages were arriving in inordinate number. It was, he discovered, the eve of my wife's birthday. He appeared visibly shattered that he had not known and had not obtained a suitable present. Then his eyes brightened. At six the next morning, his lorry arrived and, to the bitter envy of our fellow residents, removed the Matterhorn of garbage which fronted our dwelling. In parting, he left, at the front door, a simple, hand-written card: *Happy Birthday, Mrs. Axelrod.*

That's civilised.

About my American accent. I fear its days are numbered. I can only report that, though I started out sounding a bit like David Frost, I have now reached the cross-roads, heading rapidly toward the point of no return.

The best example I can give: I no longer know how to say aloud the name of those small round red things you cut up and put into salad. "To*mah*to," still sounds affected to my ear, but "to*may*to" is beginning to sound vulgar.

Pretty soon I won't have the courage to open my mouth, which may well be regarded, in some circles, as a blessing in disguise.

"*I say, Miss Tibbs, I do hope all those cars have got people in them.*"

167

"We must be nearly there—I can feel the savoir-faire."

THE EUROPEAN TOUR

More and more Americans are coming over to have a look
at Europe before it becomes indistinguishable from
America. MAHOOD records their comments

*"I'm pooped—why don't you go out
and shoot a few reels and I'll see it
all at home."*

*"I somehow thought that Britain
would be better under the Tories."*

"*If you ask me, that guy is miming.*"

"*I never realised what prime viewing time could be like without the commercials.*"

"*How do you rate on safety?*"

"***Nobody*** *sits anything out on our tours, Mr. Herman—we insist that* ***everybody*** *gets their money's worth.*"

Would YOU like to be a Special Case too?

Anyone can have a unique claim for a pay rise, if they rethink hard enough. Like, for instance . . .

Commuters

The idea has been allowed to grow that commuting is now a modern, automated, clean business. Any commuter will tell you different. They go to work miles underground still, crawling painfully along small corridors with hardly room to breathe, packed into smoky, uncomfortable trucks where they have to stand motionless for hours with one hand above their heads. Industrial accidents are still common—umbrella wounds, collapsing carrier bags, a leakage of deadly cheap scent or a sudden fall of hats—and they are bound by company regulations to absolute silence.

Conditions have admittedly improved over the years, and we no longer have the position we had during the war when men, whole families even, had to stay underground for days and nights on end. But the commuter is still a man apart, haunted at the back of his mind by the dread of that unpredictable moment when the lights go off, the trucks stop and he knows that somewhere far away men are fighting desperately to get him to safety, a fight which may or may not be won. A special case in anybody's language.

Journalists

"Now, if train drivers are going to come along and say they're special because they've got human lives in their hands—well, that makes us *extra*-special, doesn't it? I've got a report here on a man in Croydon. It's not much to look at. But when I get out the old pencil and rubber, I could with one slip ruin that man's reputation and turn him into a public object of shame. What's more, I'll be fired if I don't."

Journalism is one of the most skilful and highly specialised professions of all. It takes a lifetime's experience, for example, for a gossip columnist to learn how to rearrange his quotes and telescope the story (it's technically called "garbling") so that it simultaneously manages to infuriate the subject of the item, baffle the reader and bore the editor. A leader-writer may be at his job for forty years without once achieving the magical combination of seeing both points of view, coming down heavily on both sides, issuing a firm warning to the Government, sounding a note of alarm and realising that this much is certain. If he does, of course, it involves grave physical risk to himself.

And many newspapermen, on their own admission, encounter danger almost every time they move. They fly into war-torn provinces, use beleaguered air-strips, type this as the bullets whine outside, get their feet caught in doors and make an excuse and leave just in time. So careful do they have to be that many a political correspondent never reveals who he has been talking to. No wonder that many journalists succumb to the many occupational diseases—cirrhosis, bronchitis and loquacity. Who can look at the tell-tale bloodshot eyes and trembling hand of a journalist and not admit that here is a special case?

Waiters

"I no argue, I not complain, da miners have a special case. You go down a mine, you crash your head on da low roof, dat hurt OK. But I tell you something. In a mine you no have da smell of garlic and burnt fat. You no have crepes suzettes go 'poum!'. You no fall over little wooden tables, you no burn yourself on candles, you no have people shouting at you: 'I ask for mushrooms, you give me courgettes, you blind or something?' You not getta mad at da manager when he say: 'Fill up da glasses at number five table, or we not break even dis week', because if you getta mad at da manager, he gonna say: 'Bye bye, you go open new restaurant in Sidcup' and he know damn fine that five trattoria open in Sidcup only last week.

"So I say, we a special case. You really think I like dat da chef say to me, tell dem to have fish it going off fast? Or dat I like to give these nice people a bottle of wine dat don't know its own mother? Da kitchen don't like us, you don't like us, nobody don't like us, so I say dat's special. OK, I take your order now."

Unemployed

Probably the most special case of all. Unemployed workers receive very bad pay for doing something they haven't been trained for, a job they almost certainly didn't want in the first place and one which has a very unfavourable social image. Unemployment is a twenty-four-hours-a-day job, too, and as the work is dull routine, the effect on those involved in the unemployment industry is soul-destroying.

What makes the condition of the unemployed so scandalous is that it is actually one of our few growing industries. More than a million people are now engaged. Some towns, especially in Wales, Ulster and the North, depend largely on it for the upkeep of the community. And yet there is no adequate pension scheme, no bargaining structure and virtually no chance of promotion.

Undoubtedly this is largely because the unemployed have never unionised themselves properly and armed themselves with negotiating power. Now is the time for them to get organised, so that they can oblige the government to give a fair deal to an industry without which Britain would not be what it is today.

Cabinet Ministers

It's sometimes said that Cabinet Ministers are too well paid already, and it's true that their salary is way ahead of the minor league player or the run-of-the-mill backbencher. But the risks at the top are fully equivalent to the money involved. A star performer like a Cabinet Minister knows he is a target right from the start, and that the other side isn't going to use skill to defeat him—it's going to tackle him where it hurts, use unfair tactics, attack him when he's not looking, and do anything to get him out of the Government team. Nowadays you even find some Oppositions specially using a tough clogger or hatchet man to bring them down.

Physical contact, of course, is all part of the game, and politics wouldn't be the same without the familiar sight of one player pulling another's hair, or a team captain being beaten up by half a dozen roving backbenchers. Nobody would argue for a moment that this sort of thing should be clamped down on. But by the same token, a Cabinet Minister can receive in a moment an injury which cuts short his career for ever, as those who can remember John Profumo breaking his word or George Brown straining his credibility will testify.

Even when not cut short, a career lasts only a few years—and after only one defeat a man can often spend years in the reserves. These men are worth all the money they get, and more.

Traffic Wardens

"I've been off these last two weeks. Caught a cold in Oxford Street. There was a nasty draught between this Mini and this Chevrolet and next thing I was sneezing my head off. Not that I'm complaining. You expect industrial diseases in this job."

The traffic warden's job is probably unique, in that it is the only outdoor clerical profession. In all weathers he has to be out, filling in complicated forms. It also has a unique physical rhythm. Walk ten feet, stop, write, stoop, walk ten yards and so on. The physiomental strain must be terrific.

"Mate of mine is usually round, but he's not here today. Contracted a slight case of black eyes, actually. He had an argument with this bloke in a Triumph and lost. Mustn't grumble, though. All part of the game."

Alone among outdoor uniformed clerical workers, the traffic warden is in danger of physical assault. No-one has computed what the psychological effect must be.

"I'm lucky, actually. Haven't been done over myself. Course, had me toes accidentally stamped on once or twice, but nothing really. What I notice most is the way people look at you. Sort of as if they could kill you or run you over. Can't blame them really. You get used to it."

But what makes them a really special case is that, as a result of these indefinable pressures, they daren't ask for more money.

Still want to be a special case? Just send us your name, address and fifty reasons why you don't like your job, and we'll do the rest.

"Does this mean you'll be coming into the family business?"

THE PRESS

By SPIKE MILLIGAN

Let me take you back to India Circa 1924. (Try dialling it, you get put through right away.) It was a period when a khaki copy of the *Times* flew alongside the Union Jack at Government House. I was seven at the time. Every morning at Reveille a *Coggage Wallah delivered the *Poona Times*, which I dutifully took to my bed-ridden, dying grandfather. In those early years I thought a newspaper was something you gave to dying grandfathers. Having just read the entire range of morning papers, I am still of the opinion it is something you give to dying grandfathers. Hindu editors never quite got the hang of our language, for example, the headline:

GANDHI SENT TO YERODAH GAOL. SERVES HIM JOLLY WELL RIGHT.

and again the same week:

GANDHI THREATENS HUNGER STRIKE:
KING GEORGE VERY ANGRY GOD BLESS HIM.

I still retain cuttings of my father's theatrical exploits in India. The *Bangalore Cantonment Gazette*: "Bombadier and Mrs. Leo Milligan, the married couple, were the hitting of the night" and further on, "Mr. Bertram Kettleband did very fine readings from Charles Dickens Great Expectorations." Once a month we would receive the overseas *Daily Mirror,* in its gamboge cover.

My early knowledge of England then was through the headlines. I thought an ordinary day in England was "Heavy Snow in Cotswolds. Villagers cut off. Sheep Starving. Jimmy Wilde Champion of the World. King George Gravelly Ill. Desperate Unemployment in Wales. Gracie Fields Mobbed. Fol de Rols break all records in Eastbourne. Beheaded Nude Body of Woman found on Brighton Beach." The only normal thing in the paper was *Pip, Squeak and Wilfred.*

*Paper boy.

172

It was a shock when I arrived in England to find that people in the street were not penguins, dogs or rabbits. This made me sad, as I was a member of the Gugnunk Club. I was 13 at the time. Sitting on the train from Tilbury to London I saw the headline: DOCKS. RAMSEY MACDONALD STEPS IN.

My own father went to work for the Associated Press of America off Fleet Street, and was soon on the bottle and murmuring "There's a nasty rumour going around Fleet Street and his name is Lord Northcliffe!" During his delirium he made up headlines. "Titanic arrives safe at Southampton. 'I overslept,' says Captain," or "Arch Duke Ferdinand still alive! World War One a Mistake! 'Sorry' says Kaiser." He told me that every night City Editors knelt naked in front of a statue of Beaverbrook, crossed themselves with printers ink and said, "Please God may something terrible happen in the world tonight preferably to (a) The King, (b) The Pope, or (c) Jack Buchanan, and please God in time for the next edition, eh?"

I was 14 at the time. It's on record that the old editor of the now dead *News Chronicle* was without a morning headline and lay face down on the floor chewing the carpet. The phone rang. "Hello Dad? Brace yourself. Mother's just been killed by a coloured Chinese Jew who plays the trombone in Harry Roy's band." "Thank God," said the editor, "I'll have a photographer round in a flash." In those days, newspapers did straight-forward reporting, ie, a Football Match was reported on the merits of the game. Not so today. The reporter concentrates on the Player-Manager-Dressing Room-Boardroom conflicts. You don't report goals, you report punch-ups. A Rangers-Celtic match is now reported: "Rangers: three dead, twenty injured. Celtic: seven injured, one dead.

The unruly player gets the news. Let's take George Best. He arrives ten minutes late for practice; "GEORGE BEST MISSING! 'I don't know where he is,' says sexy 23-year-old Pop Star Sandra O'Toole, son of Peter O'Toole, who is also missing from his grave in Highgate Old Cemetary where he is making

"Mummy, Daddy—his name's Freddie. We want to become engaged."

173

'Carry on Up Your Dracula'." When Best arrives ten minutes later: "BEST GIVES HIMSELF UP!" says the midday edition. "Under questioning from hard-hitting team manager Jim 'Socks' Scrackle, 'Best broke down and confessed that he was ten minutes late'." "BEST CONFESSES! 'Ten Minutes That Nearly Ruined My Life.' Read all about it in the *News of the World*. The newspaper with its heart in your knickers." There is a surfeit of news in England, unlike my parents' bush town in Australia, Woy Woy. Nothing happens in Woy Woy. Some headlines are desperate: TODAY IS THE 3RD OF APRIL. OFFICIAL. Cub reporters try and turn minutae into leaders. "Woy Woy. April 10. This morning, during Woy Woy's rush hour, a Mrs. Glend Scrock, 64-year-old housewife, was standing at the corner of Kitchner Avenue and Bindi Bindi Crescent, when she saw a broken pencil laying on the pavement. She picked it up. It was a 2B. She threw the pencil in the gutter. The police have ruled out foul play." The fact that Harry Secombe arrived at Woy Woy station with a banner saying "I AM HARRY SECOMBE" and went un-recognised is by the way. Let's look at the character of each British newspaper each covering the same story. Let us imagine that Princess Anne, like Sir Stafford Cripps' daughter, married a coloured man, say an African goat herder.

THE MORNING STAR: MARRIAGE OF CONVENIENCE. CUNNING MOVE BY HEATH GOVERNMENT TO PLACATE BLACK RHODESIANS.

THE SUN: ITS A WHITE *AND* BLACK WEDDING FOR ANNE.

FINANCIAL TIMES: SOUND FINANCIAL MOVE BY ROYAL FAMILY. The forthcoming marriage of Princess Anne to a PAYE native Rhodesian commoner will entitle her to £100,000 from the privy purse as a married woman. Her husband's goat herd will be put in her name. The Goats will go public next year as Royal Goat Herd (Holdings) Limited.

"We were really after someone with experience."

*"I'm afraid the Howard Hughes affair rather kills **our** little scheme."*

PRIVATE EYE: PRINCESS ANNE REQUESTS PERMISSION TO MARRY WOG SHEPHERD. OPTICIAN ROYAL CALLED TO PALACE. No more coloured TV for her, says Angry Philip. When the Royal parents were informed of their daughter's wishes, the husband presumptive, a Mr. N'galu N'Goolie, was rushed to Buckingham Palace where surgeons worked on him all night with powerful bleaches. This morning his condition was described as "fair".

DAILY TELEGRAPH: COLOURFUL ROYAL WEDDING. It was announced from the Palace today that Her Royal Highness is to marry Mr. N'galu N'Goolie, a foreign gentleman with farming connections in Africa, his dark skin no doubt the result of long hours in the tropical sun supervising his herds.

THE DAILY MAIL: IT'S HATS OFF TO ANOTHER ROYAL FIRST. Our Sporting Princess is to marry a dashing dusky African goat herder. During her *Blue Peter* trip, our sporting Princess fell in love with dashing 5ft 8 ins Masai, N'Goolie Esq. A spokesman at the Palace said: "They met by accident. She ran over him in a Land Rover".

THE TIMES: Reports are coming in from our foreign correspondent that Her Royal Highness Princess Anne is unwell. Reuter.

There is no more to say about the Press. If there is, you say it.

"Whichever way you look at it the Tories are to blame. If Heath inherited rising prices from Wilson, then Wilson inherited them from Home, Home from Macmillan, Macmillan from Eden, Eden from Churchill, Churchill from Attlee, Attlee from Churchill and Churchill from that arch-Tory Chamberlain."

ARMED BEYOND THE TEETH

New York City's Assistant Police Commissioner wants his men provided with more powerful and destructive arms. "The pistol," he says "is an outdated urban weapon." HANDELSMAN is helping him with his inquiries

"Unauthorized person walking on the grass in Washington Square!"

"Things must be tough in the crook business. What does the cute little gun fire—Rice Krispies?"

"Don't worry, we'll hit somebody who's breaking the law."

*"It can hardly be called **armed** robbery, Your Honour, when my client was equipped with nothing more serious than a couple of Lugers and a Colt .45."*

"What some of the boys have in mind, Mr. Mayor, is a little incursion to smoke out the enemy sanctuaries in New Jersey, and prop up the friendly régime there."

"Regrettable, of course. We had to destroy the town in order to save it."

NATIONAL UNION OF LITERARY HUMORISTS & ALLIED TRADES

23 Tudor Street London EC4
01-583 9199

NULHAT Secretary ALAN COREN initiates a frank and full discussio

It all began (and future historians of our great movement will be quick to record the singular fitness of its so beginning) with a joke.

We were at lunch. Ostensibly a bourgeois lunch, Brothers, awash with such nob items as caviar mousse and baked courgettes and slivers of rare meats rolled in arcane veg secured with midget skewers, and served by fawning butlers besotted by a vestigial class system, or, at any rate, the folding stuff that goes with it. More, we were surrounded by a hundred and thirty years of middle-class tradition, the walls of the Punch Table Room hung with bearded Victorian comics, watch-chained to a man and indistinguishable in their respectable distinction and hair, to the point where the casual eye would have sworn that the hundred portraits were nothing but a contemporary Polyfoto of W. G. Grace.

These, however, were but the trappings and the suits of class: beneath the august ghosts and decor, as declasse a mob of modern funnymen as you could shake a slapstick at were forking down their toney scoff with an erratic energy learned in a thousand caffs and canteens and slum-school halls throughout the queendom. Most of them, indeed, still thought it was dinner they were eating. Peas flew hither and yon as the knives flashed in and out of a score of gobbling mouths, soup-stained cuffs shot across the table in pursuit of condiments and bread, and what wit there was went unheard, subsumed in the sucky din of drinking. Here was the new humorist. Keith Waterhouse, that gritty Yorkshireman, on my left, sopping up gravy like a thing possessed; Coren, the London street arab, his lap full of fallen morsels; Bill Davis, on my right, gazing in incomprehension at a fish-knife, and wondering whether or not he ought to tell Ken Allsop to

stop asking the butler for bones for his dog. Hewison blowing his Tyneside nose on his napkin.

In due course, the plates were pushed back and the burps burped; and, as the port was passed from left to right, right to left, across, back, knocked over, the discussion turned to a theme perennial among those men who have given up their lives to selfless creativity.

"Current fees for humour," shrieked one heir to Oscar Wilde, "are bleeding diabolical!"

"'Ere! 'Ere!" screamed his elegant peers.

"No bonuses!"

"No sickness benefit!"

"No overtime pay!"

Fists pale and wizened from years of typing beat the table. The Editor, not for the first time, shrank, silent.

"Dinner should be ready in three days, sir."

"What about pension schemes for writers?"

"NONE!"

"What about regularised pay-scales?"

"NONE!"

"What about paid holidays?"

"NONE!"

It was repartee of a standard not seen since the heady Victorian days of the Cafe Royal, and it might have flowed on, rich and aitchless, for hours, had Keith Waterhouse not removed a forefinger from his gum, paused dramatically, and muttered *sotto voce*:

"What about collective representation?"

Breaths were drawn in, sibilant; gasps were gasped. We were, after all, artists.

"You mean . . . ?"

"A Union!" said Waterhouse.

"Is he joking?" asked Basil Boothroyd. Humour always confuses us.

He may have been, he may not. We shall never know, now. All that matters is that there was a sort of collective dawning, a lightening of brows, one of those moments in history where all falls suddenly still and pregnant. I saw us, suddenly, marching beneath some bannered joke, our weeping headscarved wives beside us, our barefoot children bringing up the rear, our own faces grim and determined beneath our cloth caps. More, I saw Britain, strikebound and humourless, while I, blue-suited and briefcased, trotted out of Number Ten towards the waiting Humber, my lips tight with No Comment.

"I'll be Secretary!" I cried humbly.

"I'll be Treasurer!" said Waterhouse.

"The first thing to do," said Ken Allsop, "is to get some notepaper. Something headed, with a bit of class."

We put it to our first vote. It was passed, unanimously. Many hard men wept.

A week later, we had the stationery. And a clarified aim. Ours was, after all, a reasonable plea: other unions—the NUJ, Equity, the Writers' Guild—existed to serve the needs of members who might, on the surface, appear to be similar to us; but it turned out, when I chatted to their representatives, that none of them even began to appreciate the special nature and problems of the humorous trade. Prime among these is the fact that most humorists cross demarcation lines at haphazard will, into territory where the protection of their own unions, if they belong to them, doesn't operate—if Harry Secombe, say, or Robert Morley, write for *Punch*, as they do, Equity cannot negotiate adequately on their behalf when they cease to be actors. Similarly, if I write humorous copy for a TV commercial, or actually appear before the lenses myself, the NUJ

will not be able to intercede for me, should the need arise. Hence the Allied Trades of our title: ours is an inter-trade activity. Humour is its own thing, like boilermaking or foundryworking.

"What are you doing?" said my wife.

"Writing to Vic Feather," I said.

"This used to be a nice neighbourhood," she said.

"I am applying to the TUC for affiliation," I said.

"Ho, ho, ho," she said.

"They laughed at Marconi," I said.

"I can't think why," she said. "I always thought his material was lousy."

"Hey, that's not bad," I said. "Ever thought of joining a union?"

"That's not my scene, baby," she said. "I see myself pulling the tin bath in front of the fire, soling the clogs, grieving a little, that kind of thing."

I turned back to the typewriter.

"Dear Mr. Feather," I banged, "For some reason, humorists are never taken seriously . . ."

It may have been the letterhead. It may have been the moving dignity of my plea. It may have been a matter of TUC joy at the sound of new fists hammering on their door. But, whatever the cause, this is what came by return of post:

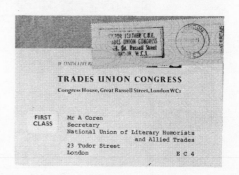

It fronted a packet stuffed with goodies, not the least of these being an extremely kind and helpful letter from Mr. Graham, Secretary of the Organisation Department of the TUC, enclosing one book, *The ABC of the TUC*, the Rules and Standing Orders of the Trades Union Congress, and an Interim Statement on the Structure and Development of the TUC, plus the information that the cost of affiliation is eight new pence per member per annum, and a request for our Rules (in duplicate) and our most recent balance sheet.

The first thing I discovered, much to my delight and relief, was that the National Union of Literary Humorists and Allied Trades, or NULHAT, I suppose it ought now be called, would by no means be the smallest union, were

179

affiliation granted it. I had been afraid all along that our members would be derided like Luxembourgers at any TUC conference, but since I have to date some hundred-odd NULHAT Brothers clamouring at my back, ours is a fairly populous gang. I learned from the handouts that, for example, the Warpdressers, Twisters, and Kindred Trades Association sports a mere one hundred and forty-four members, the Spring Trapmakers' Society only ninety, the National Union of Basket, Cane, Wicker and Fibre Furniture Makers but fifty-two, and the Shear Workers' Trade Union a scant, though doughty, twenty-five. (Indeed, I confess that my first thought on discovering all this was to make a bid for Little People's Power, drawing all these tinies under our wing to forge the mighty National Union of Warpdressers, Twisters, Spring Trapmakers, Basket, Cane, Wicker and Fibre Furniture Makers, Shear Workers, Literary Humorists and Allied Trades, to stagger the industrial world with its membership of over four hundred and an annual income running into pounds, but I thought better of it. Later, perhaps; but first things first.)

"Sitting there all day like that! What are they going to put in your biography?"

"Personally, I don't think anyone would have noticed the damp patch."

It was at this point, eager to comply immediately with the TUC request, that I made my first serious faux pas, at a stage when delicacy should have been the watchword. Clearly, the NULHAT Rules and balance-sheet would have to be shot back with all due expedition, if we were to show keenness. The Rules I should draw up myself; the balance sheet was Waterhouse the Treasurer's province.

I phoned him.

And then I phoned the TUC.

"About the balance sheet," I said. "I'm afraid our Hon. Treasurer isn't around at the moment."

"Where is he, then?"

"He's in the South of France."

There was a long silence.

"On his yacht, is he?"

"Well, as a matter of fact, I mean, I can't say for certain, but it's quite likely that . . ."

"It'll have to wait," said the voice; "when's he back?"

"In about, er," I cleared my throat, "about four weeks."

"Oh, that's all right, then," said the voice. "I'll be back from Blackpool by then, won't I? From the TUC Conference, you understand. You've heard of Blackpool, no doubt?"

I murmured something oily to calm his sarcastic waves, but it didn't seem to help much, and he rang off. I realised that NULHAT was treading among sensitive corns. I made a note to tell Waterhouse that this would be his last visit to Cap Ferat during his tenure as Hon. Treas., and bent myself to the task of Rules.

It's not easy, writing down perfectly serious,

valid points about the practice of humour; but by the end of an hour, I was done. There would be no comic writing by non-Union members: that would protect us from incursions by politicians, telly-personalities, sportsmen, and all those people who sidle up to editors at parties and tell them about This Great Idea I Have For An Article. There would be Humorous Solidarity: no more cheap cracks about, for example, NATSOPA. You should, readers, henceforth see a marked drop in the number of misprints in this paper. There would be democratic decisions on job-standards: should an editor dare to say "I don't think this is so funny," typewriters would be downed immediately, and the joke put to a vote. There would be regular Union meetings for the purposes of members telling one another off-colour stories unsuitable for print but necessary to the comic well-being of the Union. There would be a minimum of three weeks' holiday

with pay, during which time members would be safe from editors ringing up to say that As long as you're on the spot, what about a funny article on Portuguese sexual habits? There would be special rates for risqué jokes or articles involving danger of the nature of MPs' friends waylaying you outside El Vino's and hitting you with a bottle. There would be a lot of money coming our way, or else, mate, and don't give me no backchat about the state of the economy, I'm two payments behind on me colour telly, aren't I?

All is now formulated and posted. And the only thing that NULHAT still lacks to give it TUC approval is a martyr, a Tolpuddle Humorist, if you like, a man who has suffered for his beliefs. As yet, we have no candidate; but then, the management of Punch Publications Ltd. has not yet seen this article. It could well be that an appropriate martyr may be down the Labour Exchange any day now.

"Georgette, our marriage is becoming a farce."

On Her Majesty's Travel Service

By BASIL BOOTHROYD

"Greenland?" I said. "What on earth am I supposed to wear in Greenland?"

It was going to be early February when my—well, I say my—Andover of the Queen's Flight put down on the rim of the ice-cap, with about thirty degrees of frost, if my information was reliable. As an ordinary traveller you worry about clothes, especially when you're due in Florida two days later, and Mexico the day after. The pores could be opening and shutting like Venetian blinds.

My palace informant raised his eyebrows, or they may just have raised themselves, on a reflex of astonishment. Silly question.

"But," he said, as soon as he'd come to terms with my inane misconception, "you'll always walk straight out of the aircraft into a heated car." So it proved. Except that in Florida it was a cooled car. The point was that it was there. Someone recently asked Queen Frederica of Greece, exiled in Rome, what she most missed. It gave her pause. "I think," she finally said, "coming out of a building and not finding a car waiting."

Undoubtedly an honest answer. Lord Chamberlains are dispensable, also detectives keeping vigil outside the bedroom, but to find no chauffeur standing to attention with a glove on the door handle is a shaker. Particularly today, when getting from one place to another is the real killer, whether it's Epping to Liverpool Street or London to Sydney. If there's any fun to be had from hanging around airports straining for the announcements that your 747 is delayed an hour and a half . . . three hours . . . won't be flying at all, Royalty gets done out of it. When the programme says that the aircraft will depart at 0900, that's what happens, with boring inevitability. Nor are the letters ETA to be seen in those programmes. Times of arrival that are merely estimated are for you and me. (That Florida touch-down was programmed for 1610. "Prince Philip flies in on the dot," said the next day's paper.)

It isn't mere pernicketiness. Royal timetables are finely calculated, and locked on to elaborate preparations at the other end. So it's partly good manners. The Queen might be a little put out, even on her own account, to arrive behind schedule at Vancouver, Buenos Aires or Haywards Heath, and Prince Philip a little more so, the Navy efficiency streak still being strong; but they'd both be more upset at upsetting their hosts. And it's partly practical. Start even ten minutes late on one of those crammed programmes and it means a domino effect through the whole day (with rare breathing-spaces the first to go). All that aside, there's the image to think of. When the plane puts down, the car rolls into view, the Yacht warps in, on the designated minute, the waiting crowd, though they expected nothing different, thrill to the actuality all the same.

As to the clothes for Greenland, or indeed anywhere, they just don't come into it. They're there when you get there. The agonies of packing, from the

"I won them all in Vietnam except this one which I got for getting out of Vietnam."

182

"Are you sure there's a market for an agnostic musical?"

frenzied sponge-bag to a suitable climatic selection and the right ribbons on the right uniforms, are taken care of by others. There is no personal humping. ("1630: The Travelling Yeoman departs with the heavy luggage from the Privy Purse Quadrangle door . . .") And no anxieties about whether your tail-coat or favourite ball-gown is strangling to death in transit, because it hangs with everything else, secure from crush, in one of the aircraft's wardrobes. Royalty, as you may have noticed and taken for granted, emerges at journey's end with its creases in the right places and nowhere else, an enviable contrast with the bundles of exhausted and crumpled rubbish seen in the airports of the world dragging their scuffed shoes in the direction of Baggage Reclaim.

All Royal aircraft are subject to what RAF Benson calls re-roling, a word that comes off less frighteningly in print than it does on the nervous ear. It means that the insides can be torn out and reconstituted to suit the length of the trip and the size of the party. In the Andovers it happens on a lesser scale. They aren't in any case big enough for the full retinue taken on big, slap-up visits overseas, are strictly only short-haul aircraft (and turbo-prop, not full jet), and only take the punishment they do because of intensive maintenance. The engines are changed while still in their prime, and the wealth of spares would practically build a fresh aeroplane*. But a Super VC 10, say, hired from BOAC—and serviced, no doubt, with equal care—can change its internal arrangements even between flying out and flying back. Conference rooms, divans, bars, dressing-rooms can come and go, multiply or diminish.

Of the Royal Train I know nothing, except that it's used less often than you'd expect. "Overnight Train to Scotland," when it appears on the engagement card, usually means an ordinary sleeper. Given fair weather, *Britannia* is plainly the most desirable way of getting from A to B; not to say the most prestigious, a small, immaculate bit of Britain, swanning impressively around the world. I was only in her once. The routine emergency instructions in my cabin gave my boat station as "Royal Barge." Before lunch the next day I found myself automatically touching one of the many arrangements of silver-vased pink roses. Well, these days

*I was shown my Arctic survival kit at Benson, which included an animal-snare. Also the inflatable dinghy. "It's got a hood," said a cheerful Group Captain—"very nice when you're in there."

"You're right, Kate, that must be the Devlin baby."

183

you can't tell, can you? The plastic flowers are so clever . . . Again the hardships of travel are agreeably minimised. No need for any oneupmanship to get a decent table in the dining saloon or a chair in the sun that hasn't been illicitly, yet somehow unarguably, pre-empted by an unscrupulous towel; none of those hellish queues to press complaints on the harassed purser, and no swindles by the indigenous cab-drivers at ports of call (a Rolls has been swayed aboard, and gleams darkly in its purpose-built deck housing).

On the other hand, you and I haven't got to shake a thousand hands, remember a thousand names, be continuously bright at banquets. If the prospect of the Captain's cocktail party weighs heavy on us, we can always cut it. If we want to go ashore alone and sit awhile on a warm bollard, that's all right. In *Britannia*, except for actual sea time—and even then the office work goes on, and the red dispatch boxes come and go—there's no cutting anything.

Those who have been in the Royal service, and quit, come down to earth with a painful thud. They've travelled in style, by land, air and water, and forgotten the irritations and indignities of cancelled trains and unobtainable cabs, airport din and confusion and delays, the privations of the cruise ship's guided tour round the beauty spots (including those late starts and unappetising mass lunches), and after one or two ventures into the world of travel as most of us know it, they decide to stay at home.

I only had the merest sniff of it, myself. But it's surprising how quickly you get used to it. After twenty-five years or so. I can understand the Duke's darkened brow on the rare occasions when he walks out of the aircraft and finds nothing but tarmac.

It happened to me at Mexico City, after less than a week of the top travel treatment. I'd been whirled off as to the manner born at Stornoway, Keflavik, Sondrestrom, Goose Bay, Ottawa, Merida; but at Mexico City, as programmed, the Royal party whirled off and left me. It's a shock, just when you've developed a taste for the golden life, finding yourself alone, six thousand feet up, and nothing for comfort but a distant view of snow-capped Popocatepetl.

"*. . . And then came the war.*"

HOW THEY TURNED A LIKEABLE LAD INTO MR. PERSONALITY

When they picked him off the street, they found he couldn't act, or sing, or dance, or remember his lines, or anything. But he couldn't stop talking and with his set of glistening teeth, like alabaster Rennies, he was born to be turned into a star ...

The fabulous Jack Flash talks to KEITH WATERHOUSE

Shades of Michelangelo? Overnight star JACK FLASH cuts a slim figure as he steps out towards wealth and fame

The man they love to call bloody terrible reclined on a £650 leather sofa in the £24,000 rumpus-room of his £80,000 Edwardian-style mansion set in its own £200,000 golf-course, took a sip of 10p sugar-free tonic-water ("I'm on a diet") from a £1.24-and-three-packet-tops cut-glass tumbler and said:

"I know what so-called critics of the show are saying behind my back. That the real Jack Flash does not exist. That I am a tele-age Frankenstein monster created to fill a need. That I was picked up off the street and turned into a star overnight by Sir Michael Jockstrap, dynamic head of London Main Sewer Television, simply because he had a vacant 45-minute slot in his autumn schedule.

"Not a word of it is true. Nobody picked me up off the street—it was a coffee-stall on some waste ground in Fulham, miles from the road. It wasn't Sir Michael Jockstrap, although he has done a lot for me—it was his effervescent Controller of Programmes, whizz-kid Charlie Underpants. And it wasn't 45 minutes, it was a full hour.

"As for becoming a star overnight, they said that about Michelangelo. The not-so-glamorous truth is that it took me two-and-a-half days of hard graft to get to the top."

The one-time vegetable chef, night watchman, relief railway porter, Hoffman presser, swimming baths attendant, plasterer and lathman, glue-boiler, naval cadet, slate dresser, upholsterer's looker-on, apprentice cord-twiner, fork-lift-truck driver and sweeper-up in a pencil factory glanced at his £200 gold watch ("My time is valuable") and went on:

"Born? Stepney, where else? You have to be, in my job. Did I ever look round the tiny living

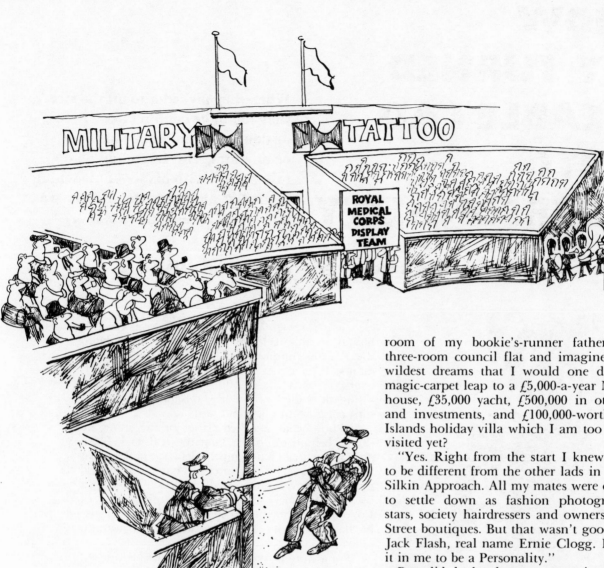

room of my bookie's-runner father's £4-a-week three-room council flat and imagine even in my wildest dreams that I would one day make the magic-carpet leap to a £5,000-a-year Mayfair penthouse, £35,000 yacht, £500,000 in other property and investments, and £100,000-worth of Canary Islands holiday villa which I am too busy to have visited yet?

"Yes. Right from the start I knew I was going to be different from the other lads in drab, treeless Silkin Approach. All my mates were only too glad to settle down as fashion photographers, film stars, society hairdressers and owners of Carnaby-Street boutiques. But that wasn't good enough for Jack Flash, real name Ernie Clogg. I knew I had it in me to be a Personality."

But did luck play any part in the runaway success story of the millionaire tele-star who once had to pawn his suit to buy food?

"Everyone needs luck in this game. And funnily enough, Keith, it was another suit—a £60, blue-satin, Savile-row job—that put me on the first rung of the golden ladder."

Let £20,000-a-year Charlie Underpants, live-wire lynch-pin of London Main Sewer Television, take up the story.

"We had had the suit made for Lennie Vest, who if you remember was last season's chat-show sensation. Then one night, just before the commercials, Lennie cricked his back while kow-towing to one of his guests, and we had to cancel his contract.

"So there we were with no show and sixty-quids-worth of suit on our hands. At the eleventh hour, just as it was beginning to look as if we'd have to dredge up some rotten old movies and fill our precious prime time with Fabulous Films of the Fifties, I found Jack Flash.

"I happened to park my £3,000 Silver Cloud on a patch of waste ground in Fulham, and there he was—heaven-sent. He was exactly the same build as Lennie. The inside-leg measurement was perfect. He could speak without dribbling, more or less. He had good teeth. Everything slotted together."

Back to Jack Flash, the council-school drop-out who made good.

"Speaking without dribbling, more or less, was the only thing they taught me at Herbert Morrison Comprehensive. But the teeth—I think they are my greatest asset—were my mother's idea. She skimped and scraped for years so that I wouldn't have to go to the National Health for my new insured-for-£2,000 choppers. Now, of course, she

lives in a £30,000 maisonette in a fashionable seaside resort. But I don't talk about that."

What of persistent rumours that the man who has everything has everything except a mother? That ex-barmaid and Sunday school teacher Mrs. Flash is an invention of London Main Sewer's publicity machine?

Jack, giving his first interview since last Thursday, pulled no punches. "If I didn't have a mother," he told me, "how could I have bought her a £30,000 maisonette in a fashionable seaside resort?"

Sir Michael Jockstrap—Mr. London Main Sewer himself—was even more forthcoming. Speaking down three telephones at once from his £50,000 pine-pannelled executive suite, he said:

"When Jack first walked into my office I could see that with the teeth and the suit going for him

"I must admit they knew their job. They left without taking anything."

he was already a considerable talent. But to become a chat-show superstar he needed three more ingredients—a mother, a gimmick, and an intimate, bang-up-to-the-minute knowledge of current affairs.

"The mother? That's Jack's own business. Just so long as she is always available to women's magazines to tell them how he still sends his laundry home and adores her home-made seed-cake, that side of the contract is fulfilled.

"The gimmick was a problem for the London

"*If only these hideous billboards weren't here . . .*"

Main Sewer think-tank. Every successful tele-personality needs some objectionable feature that will enrage the viewers and get him talked about. My boys put their heads together and came up with that brainless, hysterical laugh which is now the Jack Flash trademark."

And the knowledge of current affairs?

"He spent half an hour with me and I taught him everything I know about Ulster, Rhodesia and all those places. With a team of £20-a-week researchers to back him up—they crawl about on the floor out of camera-range and hand him slips of paper—Jack Flash could hold his own with the Prime Minister himself."

But what about stories that the wonder-boy of the goggle-box cannot even read his own name? Jack Flash himself, pointing to the rows of costly first editions lining the walls of his £10,000 library, nailed that particular showbiz lie.

"I have been able to read short words ever since I was twelve," he told me. "Anyway, you have got to remember that TV is a visual medium. You can talk twenty to the dozen about Ulster, Rhodesia and all those places and the viewers just get bored. But if you sniffle once or twice they all ring up to ask if you have a cold.

"That was the first thing I ever learned about how to make proper use of the medium. The other one was, never wear a spotted bow tie. It's been done already."

Where does the award-winning Personality of the Century go from here? What is there left to do for the man who has just hosted Britain's first round-the-clock chat show?

"I am thinking of starring in a film," he told me exclusively. "I cannot act, dance, sing, remember lines, or use my hands properly, so it would have to be something tailored exclusively for me. It could be a musical based loosely on *Hamlet*."

And if the movie moguls claimed the talents of London Main Sewer's money-spinner?

"Even a talent like Jack Flash is not indispensable," said Sir Michael Jockstrap. "We have already taught a pig to grunt intelligibly at people, and once we can persuade it to look at the right camera we plan to give it a tea-time try-out."

Caption Competition

A weekly contest in which readers are invited to supply up-to-date captions to some venerable cartoons.

"... and then I thought I'd try this computer dating."

P. Drennan of London, W.9

920 caption.—Conversationalist: "*Extraordinary crime wave we're having—er—ah—for the time of year.*"

"*I'm putting you down as a dependent relative.*"

F. E. Butler of London, SE20

1939 caption.—"*Waitah—get me a despatch rider.*"

"*Hear those drums, brigadier? It means there's a rock festival in the village.*"

L. P. Rowley of Leeds

1929 caption.—Scientist (to Old Lady): "*There are twenty million stars in the heavens.*" Old Lady (brightly) "*So I see.*"

"*Of course, I'm a special case.*"

J. Bartonholme of London, N.W.1

1927 caption.—Profiteer's wife: "*I reely ort to call on the vicar's wife, but I'm not dressed for it.*" Profiteer: "*What—not with them new furs an' jewels?*" Profiteer's wife: "*No—I wouldn't like her to see 'em; it ud only breed class 'atred.*"

NOTICE OWT SPECIAL ABOUT TODAY, FIFTEENTH OF DECEMBER?

NO LUV... IT'S RAININ' AS USUAL

YOU SWINE! YOU GREAT BLOATED SWINE!

HUSH LUV, THERE'S SUMMAT ON RADIO!

FROM MR. ALBERT SATTERTHWAITE OF GAS STREET, BLACKBURY... ..TO HIS WIFE, ALICE, ..THANKS FOR 25 YEARS OF WEDDED BLISS... SHIRLEY BASSEY SINGING 'THE LAUGHING POLICEMAN ..'

EE, LASS, YOU DIDN'T REALLY THINK I'D FORGET?

THAT'S NOT ALL EITHER! BIG DO AT THE CLUB TONIGHT. ALE'LL FLOW LIKE WATER.

SATTERTHWAITES 25th'LL BE A DO THEY WONT FORGET!

DON'T FORGET MY BIG CELEBRATION TONIGHT, ARTHUR.

I'LL BE THERE.

BY GUM, I'M LOOKING FORWARD TO CLUB. DON'T BOTHER WITH DINNER, LUV. THERE'S A MEAL LAID ON.

WHAT'S THIS? HAIR DONE! NEW DRESS!

NOT SATISFIED WI' A BLOODY RECORD ON RADIO... WANTED TO COME OUT WI' ME!

NO?

EE, WHAT NEXT?

Index of Artists

Index of Writers